EARLY LOGGING TOOLS

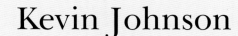

Kevin Johnson

Schiffer Publishing Ltd®

4880 Lower Valley Road   Atglen, Pennsylvania 19310

DEDICATION

To My Dad, who instilled in me the interest in and know-how for treasure hunting!

High Toppers axe and cork boots. *Courtesy of Camp 6 Logging Museum, Tacoma, Washington.*

Other Schiffer Books on Related Subjects
Cut & Run Loggin' Off The Big Woods. Mike Monte
Glory Days of Logging. Ralph W. Andrews
Logging Long Ago: Historic Postcard Views. Mary Martin, Edward Thompson,
    & Tina Skinner
Redwood Classics. Ralph W. Andrews
Timber Loggers Challenge the Great Northwest Forests. Ralph W. Andrews

Copyright © 2007 by Kevin Johnson
Library of Congress Control Number: 2007928356

Designed by Mark David Bowyer
Type set in Headliner BT / New Baskerville BT

ISBN: 978-0-7643-2740-7
Printed in China

Published by Schiffer Publishing Ltd.
4880 Lower Valley Road
Atglen, PA 19310
Phone: (610) 593-1777; Fax: (610) 593-2002
E-mail: Info@schifferbooks.com

For the largest selection of fine reference books on this and related subjects, please visit our web site at
www.schifferbooks.com
We are always looking for people to write books on new and related subjects. If you have an idea for a book please contact us at the above address.

This book may be purchased from the publisher.
Include $3.95 for shipping.
Please try your bookstore first.
You may write for a free catalog.

In Europe, Schiffer books are distributed by
Bushwood Books
6 Marksbury Ave.
Kew Gardens
Surrey TW9 4JF England
Phone: 44 (0) 20 8392-8585; Fax: 44 (0) 20 8392-9876
E-mail: info@bushwoodbooks.co.uk
Website: www.bushwoodbooks.co.uk
Free postage in the U.K., Europe; air mail at cost.

CONTENTS

ACKNOWLEDGMENTS

I would like to say "Thank You" to all of the people who have generously offered their knowledge and support to make this book a reality. To my parents, Ken and Karen, who have always been supportive of me. To my brother Ken and sister in-law Jill for their selflessness in proofreading my work and giving invaluable advice. To Dr. Don Jasted for being a mentor in regards to the world of logging tools collectibles. To Bill McDonald for allowing me to photograph his logging tool collection, and sharing his collection with all the readers of this book. To Len Hunter, a retired forest service employee, who helped me out tremendously. To Billie Howard and Charles from the Mason County Historical Museum for being so very helpful. The Adams family for sharing their interest in keeping history remembered and appreciated. The guys at Camp 6 Logging Museum in Tacoma for spending the time necessary to give me special access to the tool displays.

To Ron Jones Power Equipment, for allowing all that photography equipment to be set up during business hours. To BJ Rowland, for being the interesting guy he is and telling me, "you need that" when I pick up one of the tools he has for sale. To John Davis, who knows his vintage tools and shares his knowledge with me. To Wayne Sutton and his willingness to help me out with information on vintage chainsaws. To University of Washington Libraries, Special Collections, for their advice and access to awesome vintage logging photos. To the Tacoma Public Library, for their assistance in providing vintage photos. To Weyerhaeuser Archives for their willingness to share historical photos. To Simonds International, for their friendliness and for being supportive. To Tracy Knight, who inspired me at the start of this adventure. Finally, a big thanks to Schiffer Publishing for their interest and support in this project.

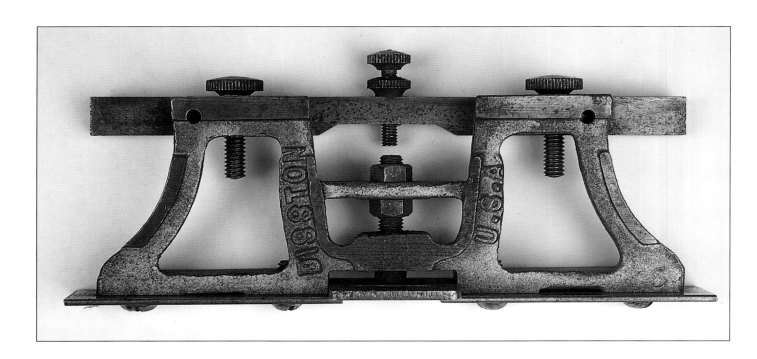

INTRODUCTION

Growing up in Washington State, I have been an avid outdoorsman all of my life. I wore flannel shirts, never used an umbrella, and found sanctuary in the woods. Known as the Evergreen State, Washington State – well actually western Washington – was once covered with a seemingly endless sea of Douglas fir. Though Douglas firs were and still are the dominant evergreen trees on the Pacific slope of the Cascades, other species also abound like the spruce, western hemlock, and western red cedar. All of these evergreens have the ability to grow to colossal size in the moist, temperate air and rich soil. I found myself in awe of the few giants that were left standing as sentinels of time. The moist forest floor of Pacific sword ferns and nurse logs filled my lungs with its rich scent with every breath I took. The forest floor also held the promise of moisture and nutrients for the seedlings that will one day, hundreds of years in the future, stand as aging giants.

My passion for nature, history, antiques, and wood working brought me to collecting old logging tools. I am sure if you are reading this you have similar interests. When I first started to collect old logging tools, I thought I was the only one. I quickly found out that I was not alone, and in fact, there was a demand at antique stores for old logging tools. My first logging tool was a crosscut saw that my brother Ken and I found at a local estate sale around 1992. While I went about cleaning off the rust, friends would ask me if I was planning on painting the saw. My, how things have changed! A nicely hand-painted saw is a thing of beauty, but it is now popular to restore a saw and enjoy it for the history that it represents.

Collection of logging memorabilia used in Washington State.
Courtesy of The Adams Family Collection. Elbe, Washington.

Great early logging photo with two fallers on springboards chopping out the undercut on a cedar and a bucker/swamper sitting at tree base.

What do the early days of logging represent? Hard work? Yes, but also a kind of romance. Old logging tools represent a day when the forests seemed endless and a man could step out of society and into another world, a place with woodsy scented breezes. It was a place where hard work was done with muscle, axe, and saw. The logger brought forth from the immense forest a needed commodity – lumber for our society to build and prosper.

Though my first early logging tool was a crosscut saw, it was my quest for a springboard that brought me head first into the world of collecting logging tools. I seemed to have always known that the notches on the sides of old stumps were springboard notches, and one day I decided it would be interesting to have a springboard. I saw photos of springboards in a 1976 Time Life book called *The Loggers*. With so many old stumps with wedge-shaped notches, I figured it would surely be easy to find a springboard for sale. I went to estate sales, moving sales, auctions, and antique stores. I took several trips around the Olympic Peninsula, all with no luck. On one of those trips I found an old springboard in a little convenience store outside of Port Angeles, but it was not for sale. No one had a springboard for sale. I would hear that they were not that common and there was a lot of interest in them and so they would sell fast. I eventually found one on eBay, and then not two months later I found two more that a tool dealer had for sale at a swap meet south of Mount Rainier. To this day, the springboard is my favorite old logging tool.

Shays No. 1 and 5 meet at Hemlock Junction. Photographer: Clark Kinsey. *Courtesy of Mason County Historical Museum.*

Saw Filer in Logging Camp, Clemons Logging Company, c. 1920s. Photographer: Clark Kinsey. *Courtesy of Weyerhaeuser Archives.*

Old logging tools hold special interest for locals where logging was a part of their community's history. Logging moved from the first saw mills at Jamestown, to the woods of Maine, the white pines of the Great Lakes states, and the pines in the South, all the way to the Pacific. The loggers and the lumber barons provided lumber to not only a growing America, but also to other countries around the world. The West grew the largest trees in the world and the loggers were quick to adapt to logging these giants. The Western falling axe, also called the Puget Sound pattern axe, came into existence with its long narrow head to cut a deep notch for the springboard to fit into. The springboard and longer crosscut saws became common west of the Cascade Range. This colossal forest stretching from southern Alaska down to Northern California was added to the forests of the Rockies, the Great Lakes states, the South, and the East Coast. Old logging tools not only saw use in these vast forests, but all over Canada and the rest of the world. Logging is a part of our history, and so are those early tools.

Small logging companies ran the show in the Pacific Northwest until the late 1800s. This was the time of the skid road and oxen teams. It was not an easy task for the early loggers of the Pacific Northwest to drag trees out of the deep, thick forests. Nevertheless, logs had to be pulled out of the woods to reach lakes, rivers, bays, and millponds. Skid roads in the Northwest were put into place around the 1850s. These skid roads were carefully built so the ox or horse teams could pull logs strung together with chain and log dogs out of the forest to the sawmill pond, river, or bay. As communities in the area grew, the end of skid roads became known as skid row because of the bars and brothels that popped up next to sawmills.

Fallers with springboards, crosscut saw, axes, and oil bottle. Usually only two fallers would fall a tree. The third logger in the background of this photo is holding a single bit axe. He was most likely ready to help the two fallers by using the poll on his axe to pound in the falling wedges behind the saw when making the back cut. Cherry Valley Timber Company, c. 1920. Photographer: Clark Kinsey. *Courtesy of Weyerhaeuser Archives.*

Great vintage photo showing logging "yarding" crew with spar tree in background. Simpson Logging, Camp 5. Photographer: Clark Kinsey. *Courtesy of Mason County Historical Museum.*

Collecting has a way of taking over a part of your life. It starts out so innocently, but before too long you might become like one of us and find yourself repeatedly looking for another place to display that newly acquired item. As time goes on the collector's acquisitions not only grow in number, but increase in quality. This book showcases some of the finer logging tools found in collections in Washington State.

You might have seen books on logging with early logging photos, but not much focus on the tools themselves. I believe this to be the first book widely published that focuses specifically on the early logging tools. It is meant to be a fun book that you will find both entertaining and a valuable addition to your library. There is a wide appeal for old logging tools: axes, chainsaws, two man crosscut saws, undercutters, stamp hammers, and others – including my favorite, the springboard.

A vender at a swap meet. Swap meets are excellent sources for antique tools. *Courtesy of BJ Rowland.*

By networking you will meet others who will trade and sell tools. *Courtesy of John Davis.*

PRESERVING / CLEANING

To clean or not to clean? That is the first question. One word of advice, do not over clean. It has taken years for a tool to gather all that age, but one touch from a stone-grinding wheel can gouge the tool, which is worse than the rust. I do subscribe to cleaning off that rust, I just believe less cleaning is best. Everyone seems to have his or her own cleaning method. I am not going to tell you how to clean up your tools, that is for you to decide. What I would like to suggest is wax, yes, wax. Not only do I use wax on wood, but also on metal. What I like about wax is that it is available with pigments that range from a light oak to a dark walnut. Wax can also easily be removed. Wax grease remover, paint thinner, lacquer thinner, and other solvents remove wax. Wax on metal not only gives the metal a nice shine, but also gives a lasting protection. I use a fine wire wheel on a bench grinder and a wire cup on a hand grinder to remove rust. A tool dealer suggested using coarse sanding discs with a hand grinder/buffer. The coarse paper for some reason is gentler than fine sanding paper. Whenever using sanding paper/discs, be very careful that you don't over clean the tool. The same tool dealer who told me about the sanding discs swears by bacon grease for wood and transmission fluid for metal.

A word about the pricing in this book. Prices given are for the tools shown in the photos. As conditions differ from tool to tool, use your own judgment on giving the tools in your own collection, or a tool that you are considering buying, a value. Also keep in mind that values fluctuate over time. The prices in this book are provided to give a basic understanding on the value of logging tools; they should not be considered definitive.

Darius Kinsey photo showing three loggers falling a cedar with crosscut saw and falling axes, Washington, 1906. *Courtesy of University of Washington Libraries, Special Collections, D. Kinsey K14.*

CHAPTER ONE
AXES

The axe is the most famous of the logging tools. Even if you have not used any other logging tools, you most likely have swung an axe. The axe, developed by early man, made its way though the forests of America, proving its utility as one of the most valuable tools known to mankind. The axe brings up feelings of independence, simple efficiency, and a winning "can-do" attitude. Though the axe has fallen considerably in the ranks of commonly used tools, it has not been forgotten by the tool collector. When axes were at their prime, manufacturers came up with colorful labels and embossed designs to set their axes apart from the rest. So today's collectors have a variety of axes to add to their collections. Just as logging itself is a part of our heritage, so is the axe, a tried and proven tool.

There are a variety of axe head patterns and weights. Some axe head patterns are very similar, while others such as the Puget Sound Falling Axe pattern is unique and easy to recognize. Whether a single bit (one cutting edge) or a double bit (two cutting edges), there are many factors that make an axe collectible. As with other collectibles, rarity and condition are paramount. Interesting embosses, original paper labels, size, and personal interest also factor into what axe to collect and how much to pay.

Nice display of falling axes against a cedar lined wall. *Courtesy of William D. McDonald.*

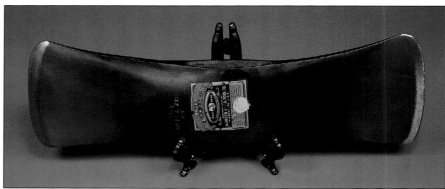

Puget Sound Pattern Sager Chemical Axe dated 1941. Sager axes were made by Warren Axe & Tool Co. This axe not only has a front label, but has on the other side an award label. Sager Chemical Axes were dipped in lacquer to prevent rust and to show off their tempered edges, which make a quality axe. 13 1/8" long. $300-400.

Back side of 1941 Sager axe head with label that touts the awards won at the Panama-Pacific and Alaska-Yukon Expositions. Not all axes came with paper labels and the ones that did are hard to find since the labels would quickly wear off.

Plumb 4.2 lbs. axe head, 13" long by 3 1/2" at cutting edges, c. 1948. $50-75.

Knot Klipper 4.2 lbs., 13 1/2". Made by Mann Edge Tool Company, Lewiston, Pennsylvania. With original drop tag. $150-225.

Colonial 3.2 lbs., 11 1/4". Sold at the Seattle hardware store Schwabacher's, c. 1930. $125-175.

Collins & Company Hartford Legitimus 4 lbs., 12 1/2". With Crown, Arm, and Hammer logo. $65-95.

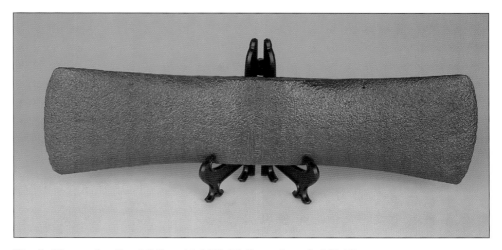

Wards Master Quality 4.2 lbs., 13 1/2". Well weathered. $45-75.

Kelly Hand Made, 13" long. $65-100.

Lumberjacks falling a tree. *Courtesy of Tacoma Public Library.*

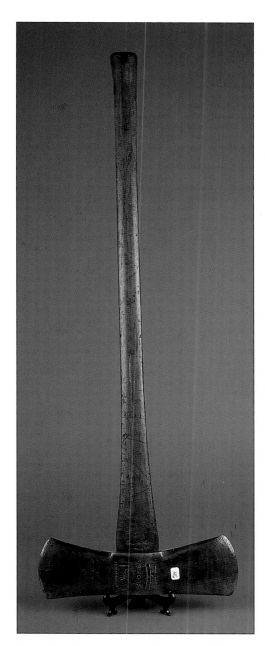

Colonial "Rings For Quality," 12 1/2" long head. $175-275.

Close up of Liberty Bell logo on Colonial axe.

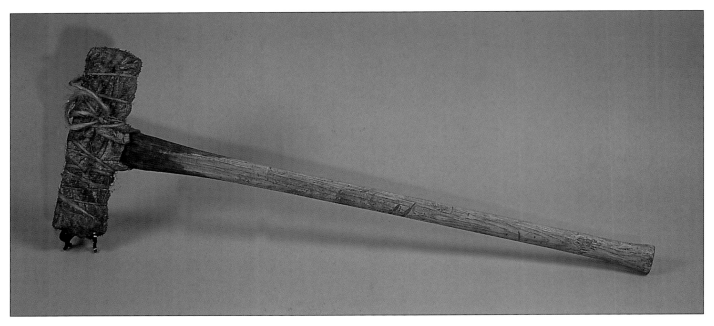

Mystery falling axe wrapped in oil soaked burlap. *Courtesy of Mason County Historical Museum.* $45-95.

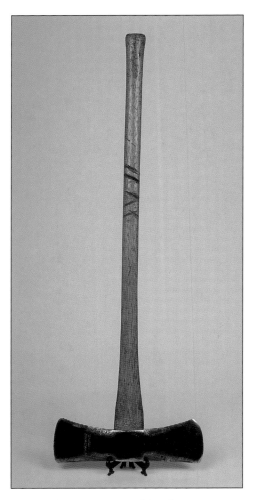

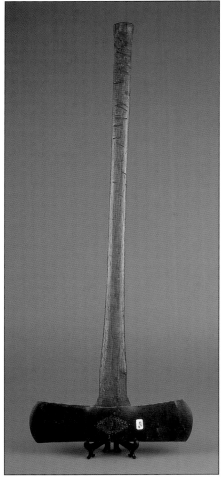

Knot Klipper Warrented by the Mann Edge Tool Company 4.2 lbs., 13 1/4" with 38 1/2" handle. Handle has under cutter notches from the axe used to support the back of a bucking saw while sawing a log from the underside. $125-175.

Occident Seattle Hardware Co. 12 3/8" head with a 33" long handle. $135-175.

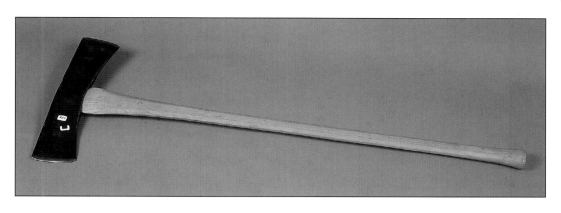

White Stub & Twist GWA. Honse-dale, Pennsylvania. Though rough in its casting, White axes are hard to find and are quite collectible. 14 5/8" long head, octagon handle 40 1/2". $300+

Catalog listing for Sager double bit axes.
Courtesy of Dr. Donald C. Jastad.

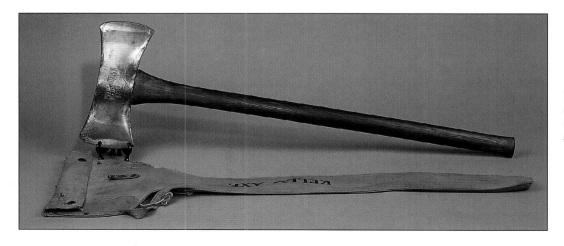

Kelly Signature axe with rare Kelly marked full sheath. *Courtesy of William D. McDonald.*

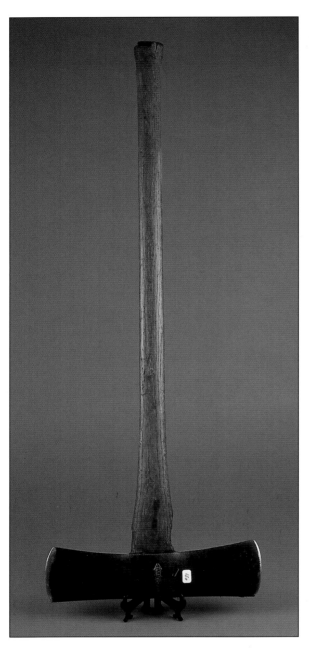

**Stiletto axe sold by Baker Hamilton & Pacific Co.
$95-150.**

Close up of Stiletto axe.

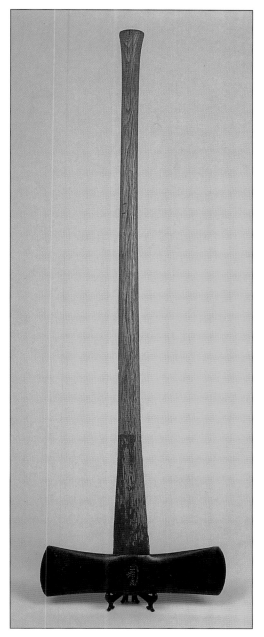 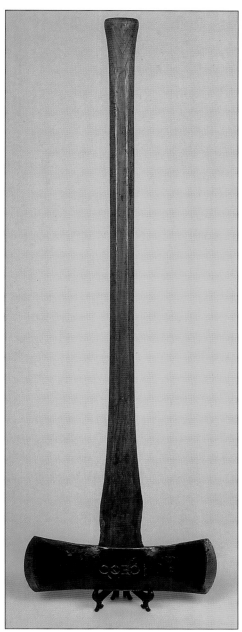

Zenith 4.2 lbs., 13 1/4". Zenith was Marshall Wells Company's top brand. The long slender handle measures 42". The paint on the handle probably meant this axe belonged to a logging company, c. 1940. $100-175.

Ceco 4.1 lbs., 11 5/8", c. 1920. Clyde Equipment Co. Portland, Oregon. Octagon handle. $65-95.

Close up of Zenith axe.

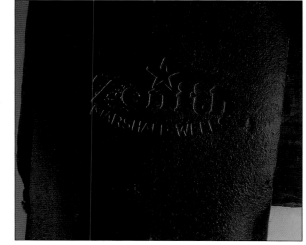

Close up of Ceco axe.

19

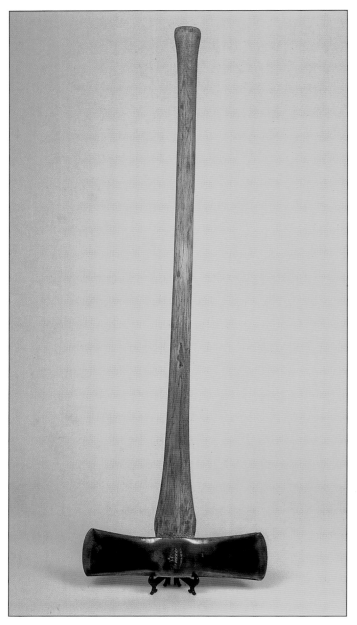

Zenith 4.2 lbs., 13 3/8". Handle 41 3/4" long. Later version with all capital letters, c. 1950. $125-175.

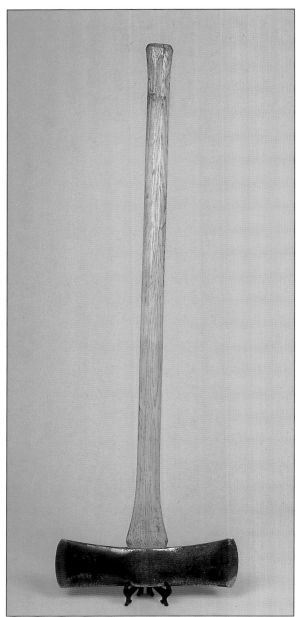

Rare Red Knight axe 12 1/4". Replacement octagon handle 37 1/2". $85-165.

Close up of Zenith axe. The logos of Zenith axes changed over the years.

Close up of Red Knight axe.

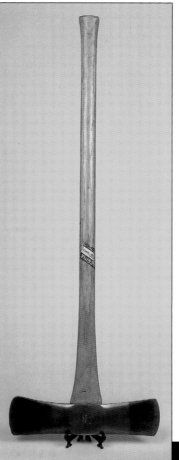

True Temper Flint Edge 4.2 lbs., 13 3/4" with a 39 3/4" handle. Hard to find heads of this length. $125-165.

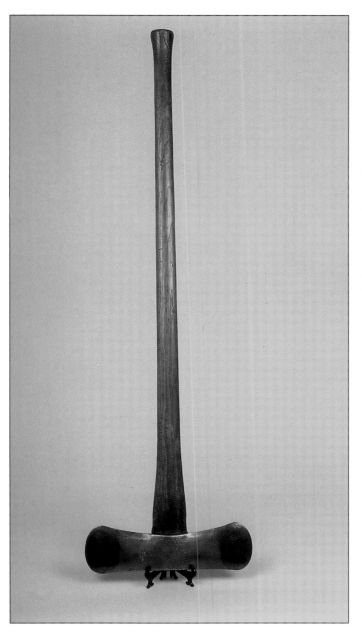

Close up of True Temper Flint Edge axe.

The Sager axe was favored by many loggers. Nice patina on this Sager Chemical Axe dated 1934. 12 1/2" inch head with a 42" handle. $75-145.

Close up of the Bruner Ivory Handle Co. Hope, Arkansas, label.

High climber/topper with gear. The rope the high climber used around the tree had a metal wire core to help prevent accidentally cutting through the rope when using the axe. Weyerhaeuser Timber Company, Vail McDonald, WA. Branch. c. 1940s. Photographer: unknown. *Courtesy of Weyerhaeuser Archives.*

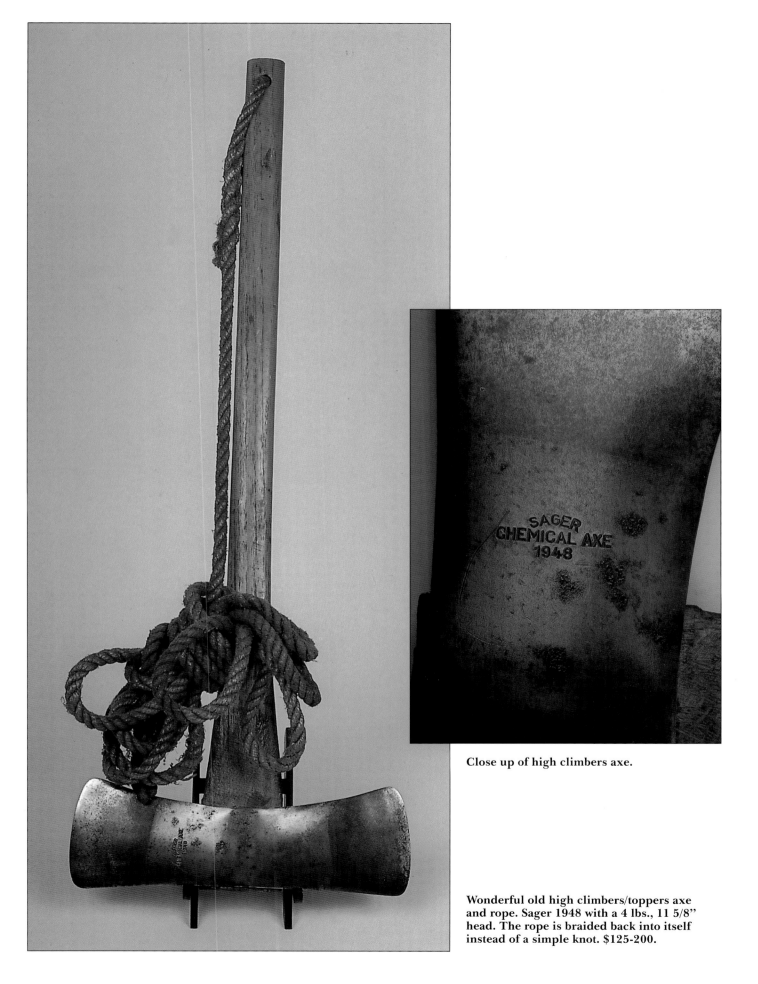

Close up of high climbers axe.

Wonderful old high climbers/toppers axe and rope. Sager 1948 with a 4 lbs., 11 5/8" head. The rope is braided back into itself instead of a simple knot. $125-200.

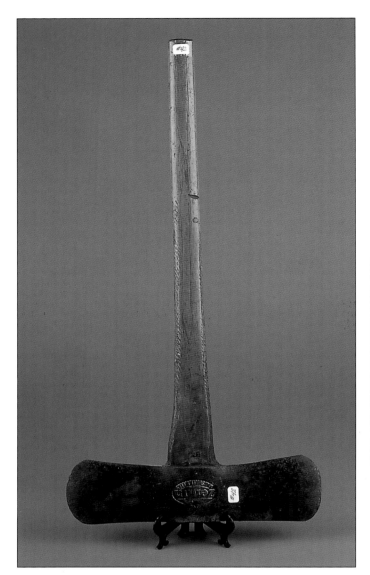

Zenith axe with short handle. 12 1/8" head with a 23 3/4" handle. $65-100.

Close up of high climbers axes; 13", 4.2 lbs. plumb, and 12 1/2", 4.2 lbs. 1936 Sager.

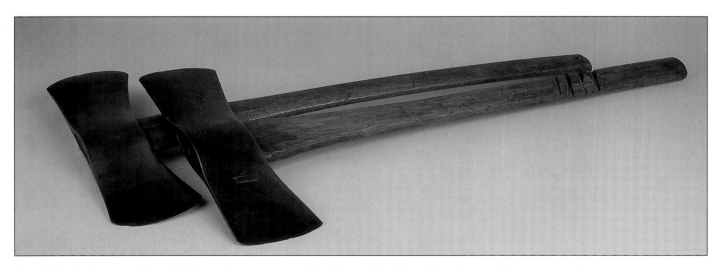

Two high climber axes. The 1936 Sager has an octagon handle, and the Plumb has deep undercutter notches.

Logging crew including high climber/topper. The high climber would let his axe and saw hang down below him so they would be out of his way. The saw and axe were attached to his climbing belt with ropes about ten feet in length. Camp 1, Simpson Logging Company. Photographer: Clark Kinsey, 1924. *Courtesy of Mason County Historical Museum.*

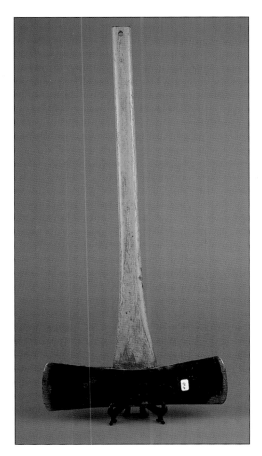

Beautiful 4 lbs. plumb high climber/ toppers axe. $85-145.

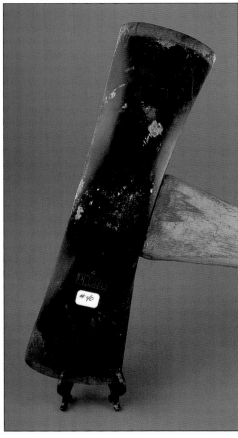

Close up of plumb high climber/topper with most of its original black finish.

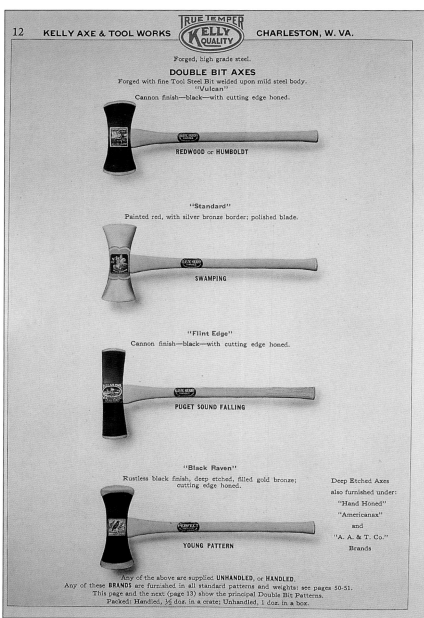

Kelly Axe & Tool Works double bit axe listing.
Courtesy of Dr. Donald C. Jastad.

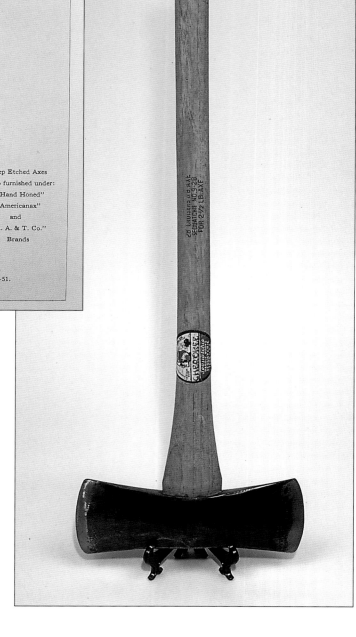

Little unmarked cruiser type double bit
with Cherokee labeled handle. Head
measures 8 7/8" and the Sequatchie
handle measures 26 1/2". $35-75.

Kelly True Temper Black Raven cruiser with nice patina handle. $95-150.

Close up of the Black Raven logo with some wear to logo.
Black Raven is a favorite among collectors.

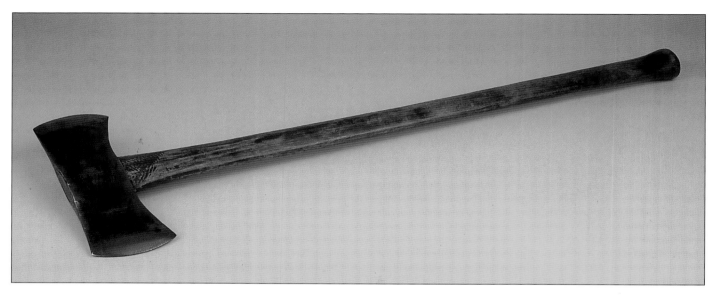

Mann Edge Tool Co. 9 1/2" head with a 32" handle. USFS and CCC stamped. $40-80.

Close up of Mann axe. The abbreviations USFS and CCC stand for United States Forest Service, and Civilian Conservation Corp. This one is stamped a number of times.

Two nice little cruiser axes, both are Plumbs. $45-75 ea.

Close up of the two cruisers. Notice that even though they are both Plumbs they have different heads. Both measure 8 1/2" in length, but are different in the width of their cutting edges. The black Plumb has cutting edges that measure 4 1/4" and the silver Plumb 3 3/4".

Vintage photo of three loggers with axes, saw, oil bottles, and springboards.

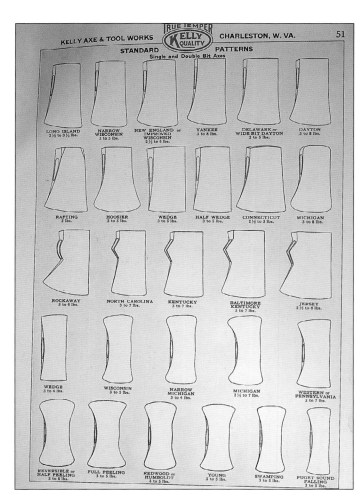

Single bit and double bit axe patterns.
Courtesy of Dr. Donald C. Jastad

Close up of the nice Cut Easy logo.

Nice example of a Cut Easy Smith Bros. H.D.W. Co. Columbus, Ohio. In the Michigan pattern. $75-125.

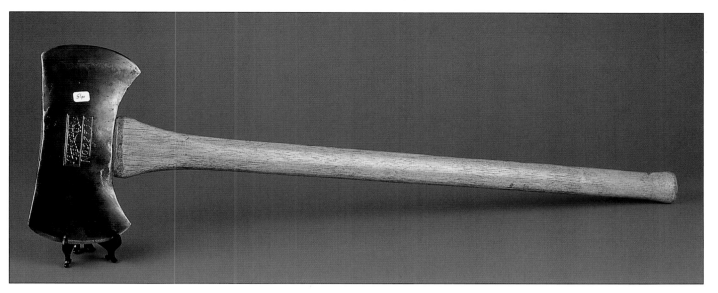

Kelly Registered Axe. These were individually numbered. $75-125.

Close up of Kelly registered with serial number etched into blade.

Sager axe head 5 lb. Most double bits (having two cutting edges) axes were stamped with a number signifying their weight; 3.4, 4, and 4.2 lbs. are most common. This one is a 5 lb., which is not often seen. $35-75.

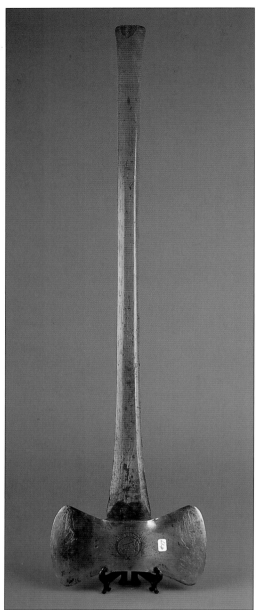

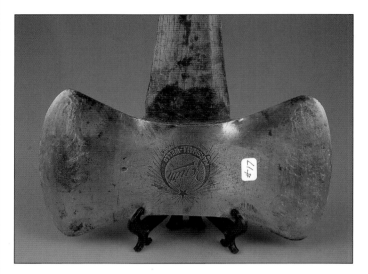

Close up of early Zenith logo.

Zenith Marshal Wells with early star burst
logo. $95-135.

Hard to find Collins
Legitimus with
unusual logo.
$125-160.

Close up of Collins logo
with Crown, Arm, and
Hammer.
The Collins Company,
Collinsville, Conn.

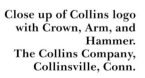

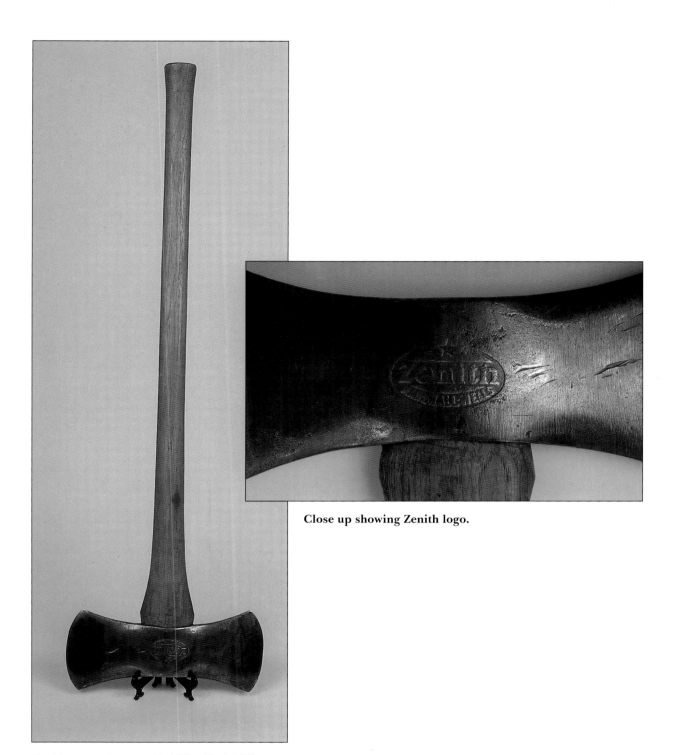

Close up showing Zenith logo.

Zenith swamping axe 10 1/2" with 4 1/2"
cutting edges. Heavier 34 1/4" handle. $65-95.

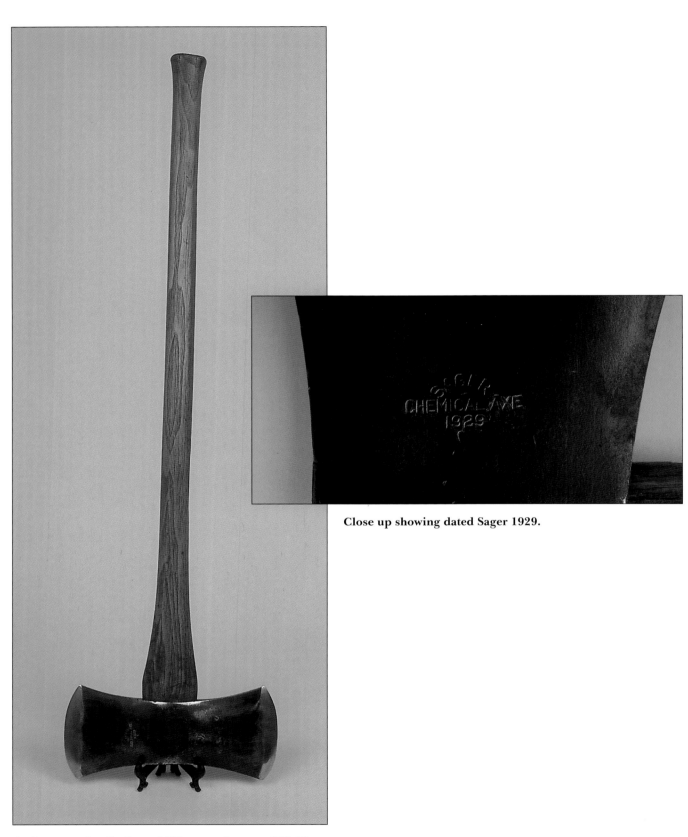

Close up showing dated Sager 1929.

A nice example of a Sager 1929 swamping axe. $65-95.

Winchester 9 1/4” x 5” with a nicely patina 34” handle. $125-185. *Courtesy of John Davis.*

Close up of Winchester stamping. *Courtesy of John Davis.*

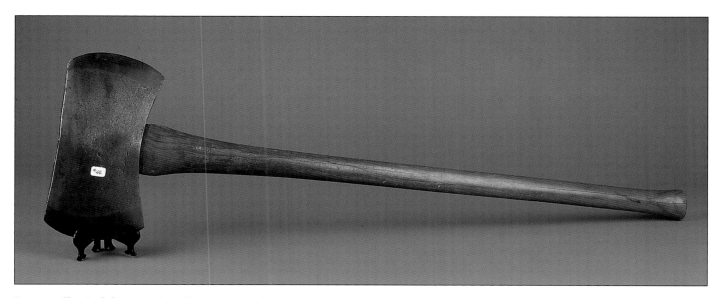

Rare peeling/sniping axe, 5 1/4” x 10 1/2”, with a 6.2 lbs. head. Primarily used to peel off the thick bark from trees like the Douglas fir. $125-195.

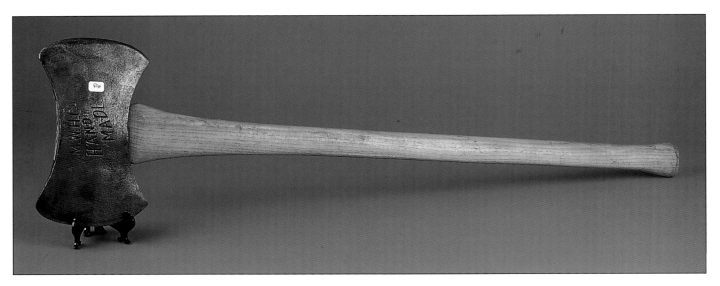

M.W.H. Co. Hand Made, Marshal Wells Hardware Company.
$45-95.

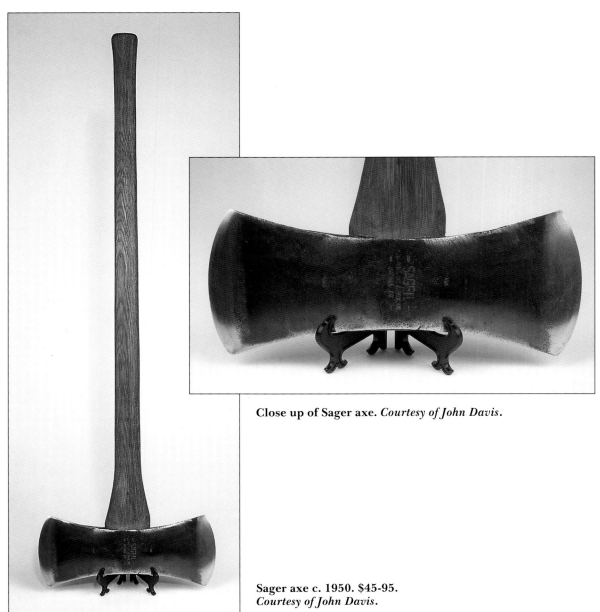

Close up of Sager axe. *Courtesy of John Davis.*

Sager axe c. 1950. $45-95.
Courtesy of John Davis.

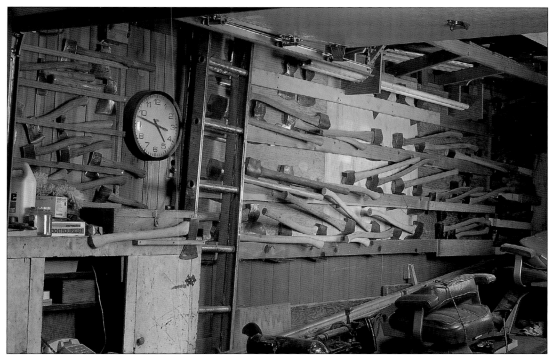

Single bit and broad axes line the wall. *Courtesy of John Davis.*

Warren Axe & Tool Company. Chainsaw/Undercutter axe head with wooden box printed; 1/2 doz. Warren Axe Anti Rust Undercutter. $65-120.

Collins Legitimus Chainsaw/Undercutter axe. These axes were developed for use with the early chainsaws. The early chainsaws cut the undercut notch, and the Chainsaw/Undercutter axe was then used to remove the wood wedge. $65-120.

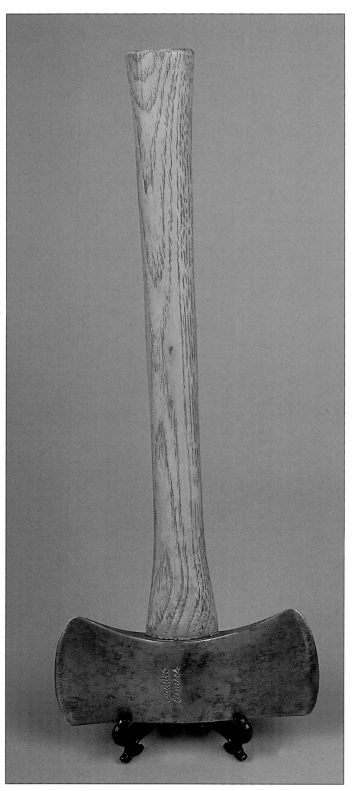

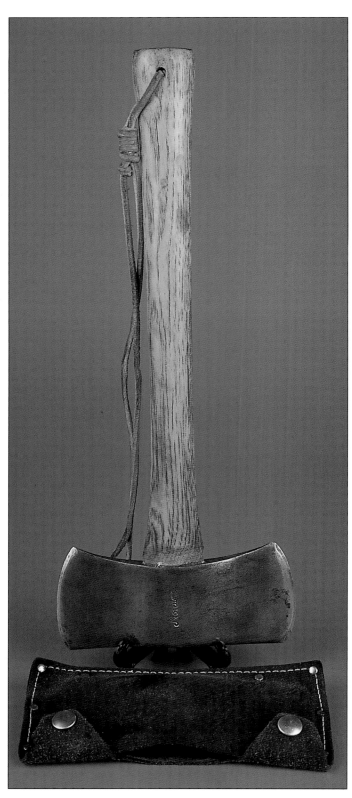

Saddle cruiser axe. $100-185.
Courtesy of William D. McDonald.

Norlund cruiser axe with Norlund marked sheath. 6 3/16"
with a 15" handle. $100-175.

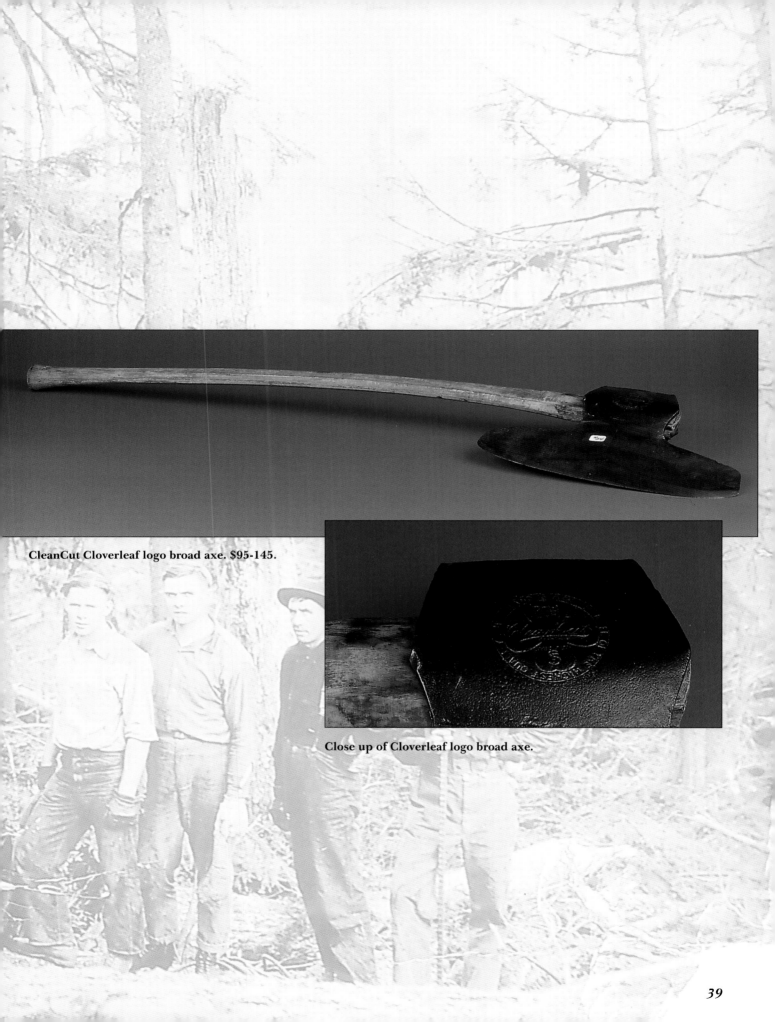

CleanCut Cloverleaf logo broad axe. $95-145.

Close up of Cloverleaf logo broad axe.

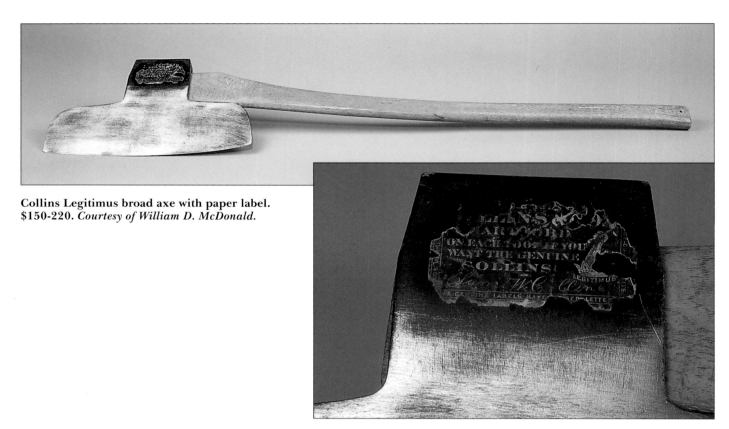

Collins Legitimus broad axe with paper label.
$150-220. *Courtesy of William D. McDonald.*

Close up of Collins Legitimus broad axe paper label. Axes with original labels are uncommon. *Courtesy of William D. McDonald.*

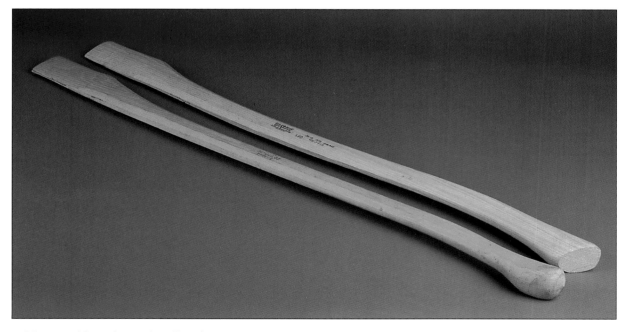

NOS (new old stock) axe handles. $35-55.

Close up of hatchets with nice logos. *Courtesy of John Davis.*

Plumb 7 3/8" broad axe with shortened handle. Notice the cuts added to the handle by a previous owner for a better grip. $65-95.

Rare cable/wire axe. The splayed end was pounded into a log and the cutting edge used to cut cable. $95-165.

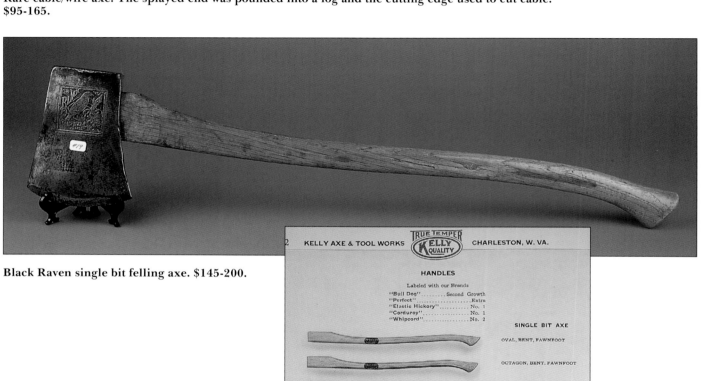

Black Raven single bit felling axe. $145-200.

Kelly Axe handle illustration
from early tool catalog.
Courtesy of Dr. Donald C. Jastad.

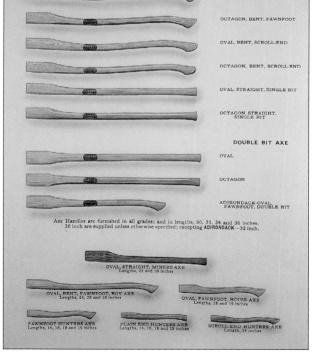

Close up of Keen Kutter logo.
Courtesy of John Davis.

Keen Kutter felling axe. $45-75.
Courtesy of John Davis.

Uncommon Van Camp single bit axe. $45-75.

Close up of Van Camp axe. 100 BBB A nice example of a OVB (Our Very Best) axe. $35-85.

CHAPTER TWO
SAW IT

The two man crosscut saws are long saws that represent a time of big trees and never-ending thick forest. It is a simple looking tool, but one that needs to be used and tuned correctly to avoid being "a misery whip." Two man crosscuts saws at first seem to be saws of the past, no one uses them anymore. Not true! The U. S. Forest Service uses crosscut saws in the national forests, and competition crosscut saws are used at lumberjack shows.

Crosscut saws come in a variety of lengths and tooth patterns. The longest saws, the ones used for the redwoods, were manufactured up to twenty feet in length. Saws that are in good shape, with visible logos, little rust, and long teeth command high prices. Certain names such as Simonds Royal Chinook are very popular among both collectors and users of the two man crosscut saw. There are also a number of handle styles for crosscut saws, with the western, climax, and loop as the most common.

Saw filing is an art and one that takes time to develop. Loggers depended on the skilled logging camp saw filers to keep their saws in tiptop shape. Saw filing tools are not only sought after by collectors but by today's saw filers.

SAWS

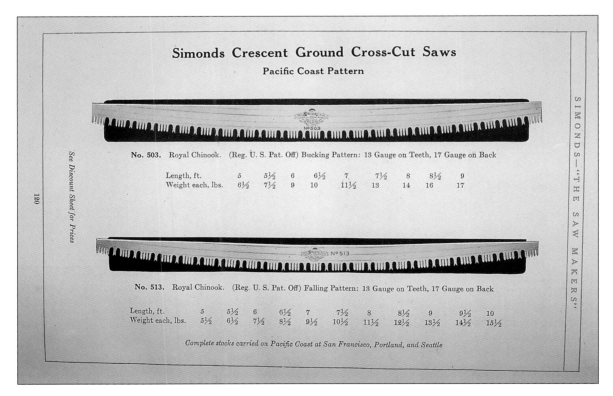

Simonds illustration showing Pacific Coast pattern Royal Chinook falling and bucking saws.
Courtesy of Simonds International.

High up on their springboards, and before starting the undercut, two fallers pose to have their photo taken. Clemons Logging Company, c. 1920s. Photographer: Clark Kinsey.
Courtesy of Weyerhaeuser Archives.

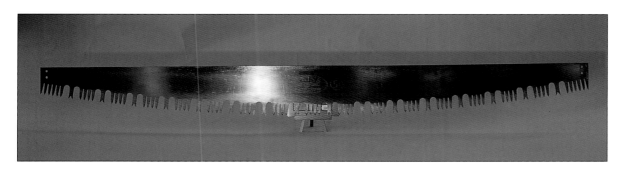

Atkins Silver Steel No.51 bucking saw. $250-350. *Courtesy of Dr. Donald C. Jastad.*

Close up of Atkins No.51 bucking saw. *Courtesy of Dr. Donald C. Jastad.*

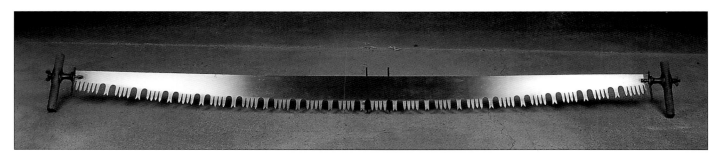

Nice example of an early Simonds Royal Chinook 513 falling/felling crosscut saw, 8' long, a favorite of loggers in the Pacific Northwest. $200-275.

Close up of Simonds Royal Chinook 513 logo.

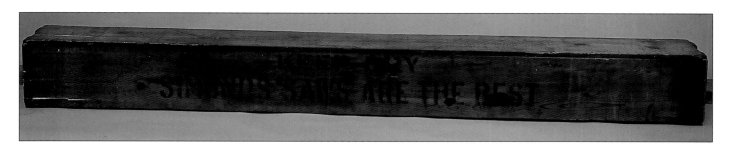

Rare Simonds crosscut saw box, 7' 10". Sent to Olympia Supply Co. Washington. $75-150.

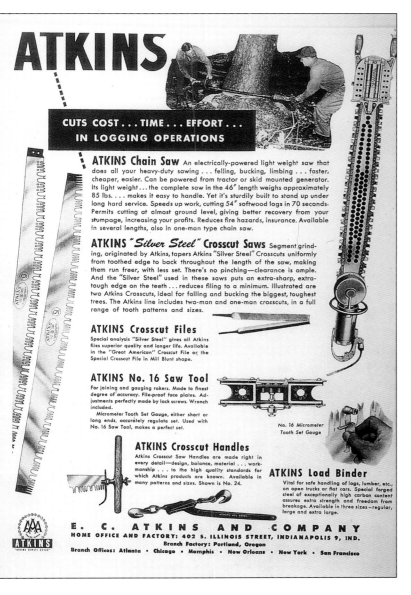

E.C. Atkins & Company advertisement.
Courtesy of William D. McDonald.

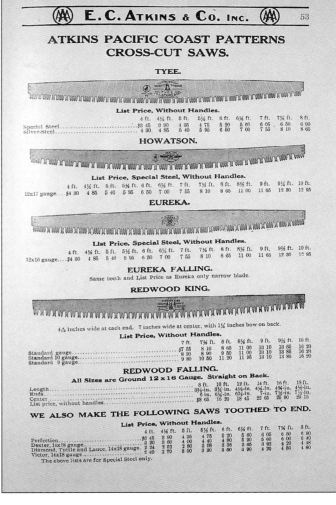

Atkins illustration showing Pacific Coast patterns. *Courtesy of Dr. Donald C. Jastad.*

Rare three piece Atkins Take-Down 6' 6" falling/felling saw with canvas carrying case made for use by the U.S. Forest Service. $400-550.

Close up of the Atkins 52 logo and U.S. Forest Service stamp on Take-Down Saw.

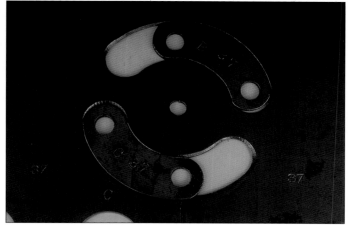

Close up of the well made cam levers that tie the three piece saw together. Notice how each lever is stamped with a letter and a number that corresponds with the letter and number on the saw blade.

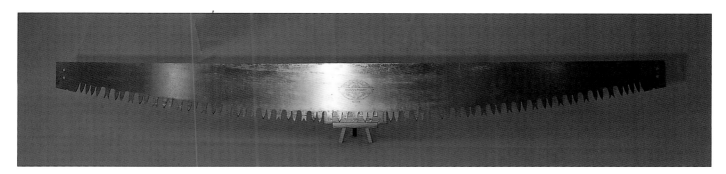

Geo. Worthington Co. Anniversary bucking saw. $150-200. *Courtesy of Dr. Donald C. Jastad.*

Close up of Geo. Worthington Co. Anniversary No. 1418 bucking saw. *Courtesy of Dr. Donald C. Jastad.*

Atkins three piece Take-Down falling/felling saw 5' 6" with canvas carrying case, spanner wrench, and a handle. $400-550. *Courtesy of William D. McDonald.*

Close up of Atkins 52 logo with U.S. Forest Service stamp, and canvas carrying case in background. c. 1930. *Courtesy of William D. McDonald.*

Brothers James and Bill (William) McDonald. Coming from a family of twelve kids, ten of who were boys, both James and Bill, along with their eight other brothers, worked in the woods, following in the steps of their father. In the background, NOS drag saw blades, crosscut saw vises, oil bottles, and axes. *Courtesy of William D. McDonald.*

Close up of NOS Atkins Paul Bunyan 1 Drag Saw. *Courtesy of William D. McDonald.*

Close up of NOS Atkins Paul Bunyan 1-4 Drag Saw. *Courtesy of William D. McDonald.*

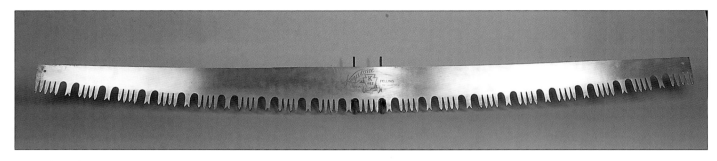

Very nice Disston Keystone K462 crosscut falling/felling saw 6' 6". $175-250.
Courtesy of William D. McDonald.

**Close up of Disston
Keystone saw with
strong logo.** *Courtesy of
William D. McDonald.*

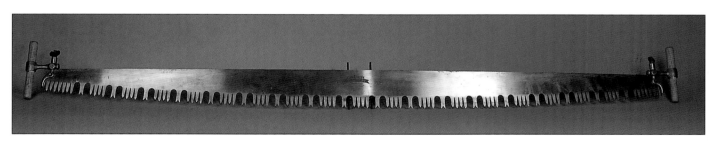

A nice example of a later Simonds Royal Chinook No.513 falling/felling saw. Over the years Simonds
changed the look of their logo. $200-275. *Courtesy of William D. McDonald.*

Logger bucking logs for Weyerhaeuser Timber Company, Snoqualmie Falls, WA. Branch, c. 1949. Photographer unknown. *Courtesy of Weyerhaeuser Archives.*

Disston No. 7-11 falling/felling crosscut saw. Besides the Disston marks, this saw is also stamped CCC (Civilian Conservation Corps 1933-1942) S-D-F (State Department of Forestry) and U.S. Forest Service. A very interesting saw. $275-375. *Courtesy of The Adams Family Collection, Elbe, Washington.*

Close up view showing Disston logo and U.S. Forest Service stamp.
Courtesy of The Adams Family Collection, Elbe, Washington.

**Close up of the CCC and
S-D-F stamps.** *Courtesy of The
Adams Family Collection, Elbe,
Washington.*

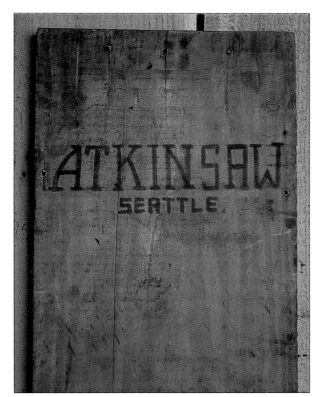

Atkin Saw stamped board (from
a wooden saw box). *Courtesy of
William D. McDonald.*

Board from a wooden box
that held Drag Saws. *Courtesy
of William D. McDonald.*

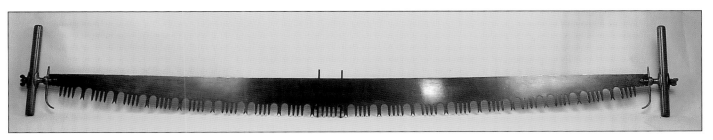

Nicely restored 7' crosscut saw. Loggers frequently would snap off the end teeth from each end of the saw.
These teeth were not needed and loggers preferred the teeth out of the way. $100-175.

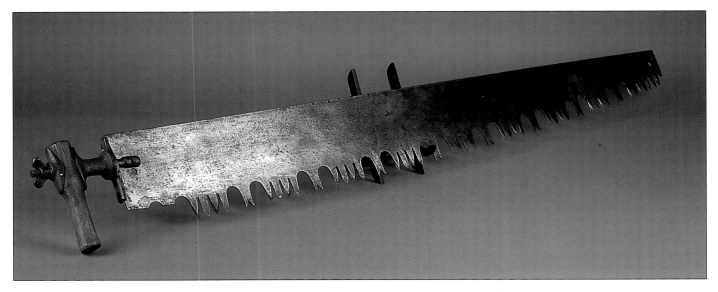

High toppers saw. The high topper would tie a rope around the handle or sometimes drill a hole in the
handle for the rope. He would then let the sharp saw hang down about five to ten feet below him as he
climbed the tree. The saws used were typically saws that had snapped. The high topper only need a saw
about four feet in length. $85-125.

Tuttle tooth 4' Disston No. 208. $95-150. *Courtesy of William D. McDonald.*

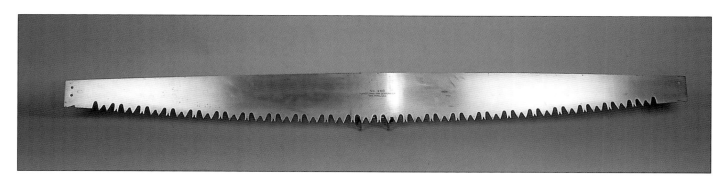

6' Pennsylvania No. 960 hardwood saw. $95-150. *Courtesy of William D. McDonald.*

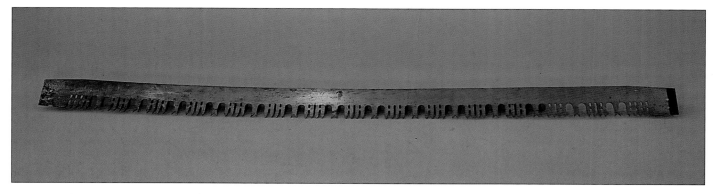

Lance tooth eastern crosscut saw. $75-125. *Courtesy of Dr. Donald C. Jastad.*

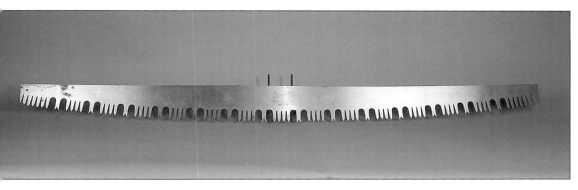

Ohlen Bishop No. 252 6' crosscut saw. $275-350. *Courtesy of William D. McDonald.*

Close up of Ohlen Bishop saw. Notice the long teeth, which are found on saws that have not been filed. *Courtesy of William D. McDonald.*

Saw vise with saw hanging from the rafters of a saw shop near Mount Rainer. $100-185. *Courtesy of The Adams Family Collection, Elbe, Washington.*

Three long falling/felling crosscut saws. The bottom saw blade measures 8' 6" with a nice pair of Simonds Royal Chinook marked handles. The middle saw was originally a 10' saw, but each end was snapped off to make a 9' 6" saw. The top saw is a ten-footer. Most falling/felling saws have handles that were cut down by the logger. Loggers liked using shorter handles when standing on springboards. Supposedly, the longer the handle, the likelier of snagging the handle on one's suspenders.

Long one man crosscut saw with helper handles, 5' 6" blade. $55-95.

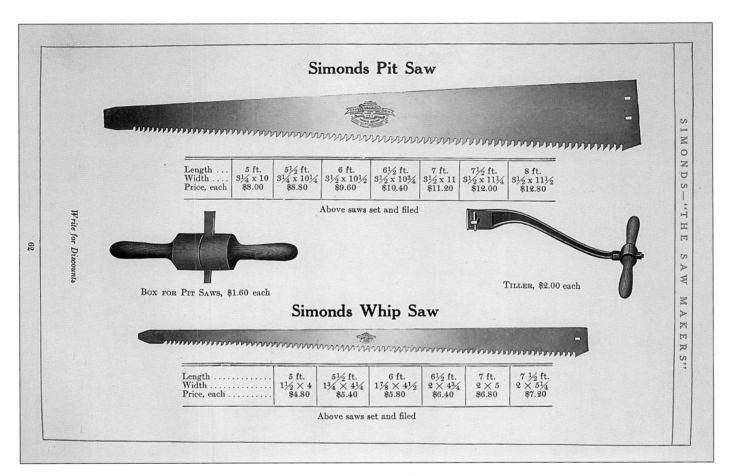

Simonds Pit Saw

Length ...	5 ft.	5½ ft.	6 ft.	6½ ft.	7 ft.	7½ ft.	8 ft.
Width	3¼ x 10	3¼ x 10¼	3½ x 10½	3½ x 10¾	3½ x 11	3½ x 11¼	3½ x 11½
Price, each	$8.00	$8.80	$9.60	$10.40	$11.20	$12.00	$12.80

Above saws set and filed

Box for Pit Saws, $1.60 each

Tiller, $2.00 each

Simonds Whip Saw

Length	5 ft.	5½ ft.	6 ft.	6½ ft.	7 ft.	7 ½ ft.
Width	1½ × 4	1¾ × 4¼	1⅞ × 4½	2 × 4¾	2 × 5	2 × 5¼
Price, each	$4.80	$5.40	$5.80	$6.40	$6.80	$7.20

Above saws set and filed

Write for Discounts

62

SIMONDS—"THE SAW MAKERS"

Simonds illustration showing Pit saw and Whip saw. *Courtesy of Simonds International.*

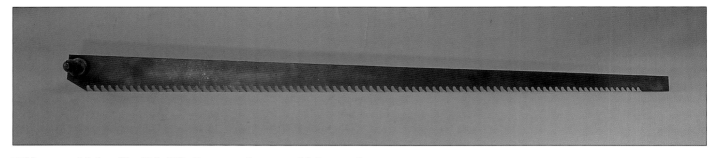

Whip saw with handle. $95-175. *Courtesy of Dr. Donald C. Jastad.*

Bucker crosscutting large spruce. *Courtesy of University of Washington Libraries, Special Collections, D. Kinsey A47.*

HANDLES

Large wooden box filled with an assortment of two man crosscut handles.
Courtesy of William D. McDonald.

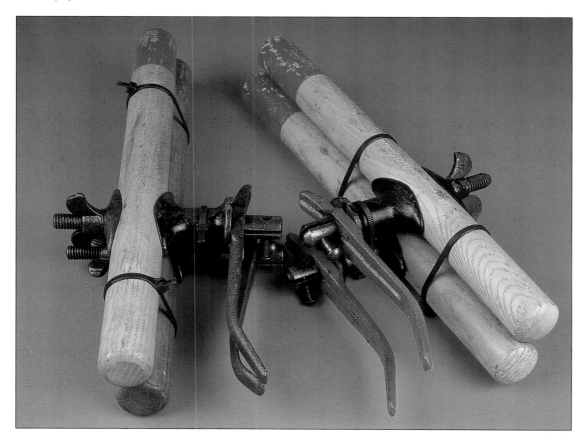

Simonds Royal Chinook 395 handles in almost new condition.
$75-125 a pair.

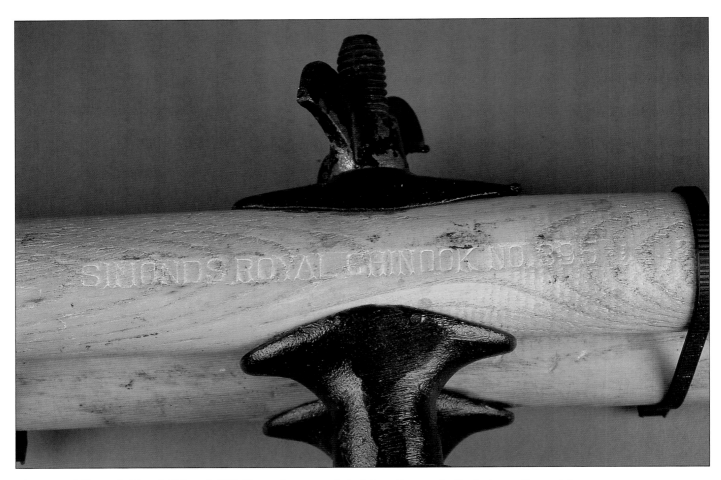

Close up of Simonds Royal Chinook 395. Simonds stamped their handles vertically between the metal hardware. Atkins and Disston stamped their handles horizontally on the upper quarter of the handles. Each manufacturer made a number of handle styles.

Used pair of Simonds Royal Chinook western saw handles.

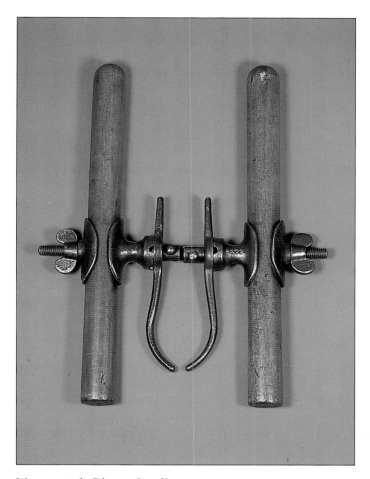

Western style Disston handles.

Western style Atkin handles.

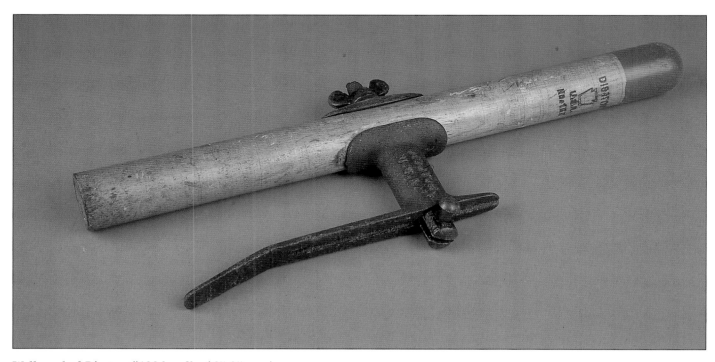

Well marked Disston #128 handle. $65-95 a pair.

Atkins Silver Steel No. 24 two man saw crosscut handle. $65-95 a pair.

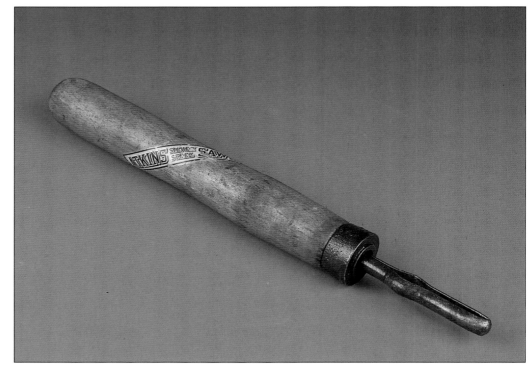

Atkins Silver Steel East Coast style two man crosscut saw. $45-85 a pair.

Universal handle, 13 7/8". $45-85 a pair.

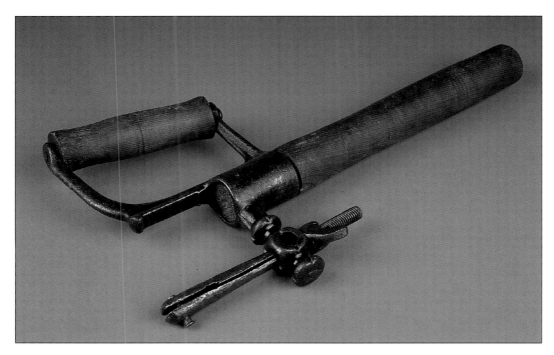

Rare bucking handle 14 1/2". $75-100 a pair.

Nice pair of Atkins 52 falling handles 8 1/4" long. $55-95.

Victor made in Canada falling and bucking saw handles. The shorter one is a falling/felling handle and the longer one is a bucking handle. $60-95 a pair. *Courtesy of William D. McDonald.*

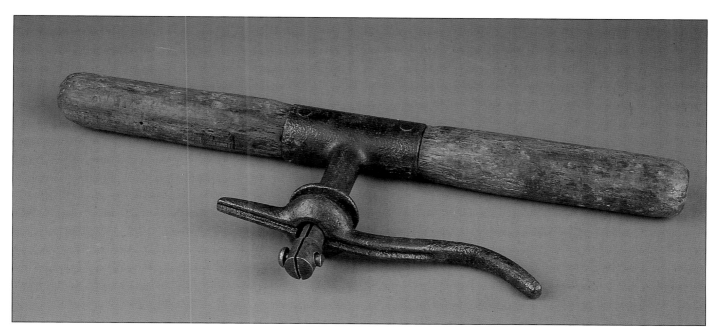

Unusual saw handle. Pat. Jan. 1, 07. $60-95 a pair.

Pair of early bucking handles. $45-80 a pair.

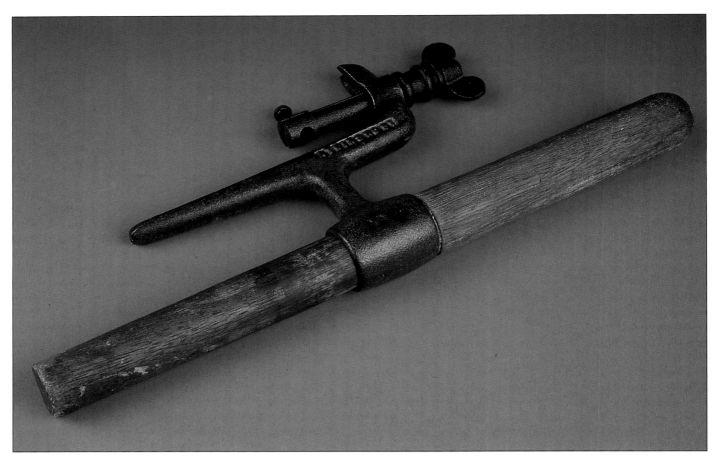

Atkins bucking handle No. 51 bucking. $60-95 a pair.

Atkins Pacific Coast handle No. 30 bucking. Metal hardware made of aluminum with a steel bolt and wing nut. $75-125 a pair. *Courtesy of William D. McDonald.*

John Sells handle. $60-95 a pair.
Courtesy of William D. McDonald.

FILING TOOLS

Display of filing tools on cedar lined wall. *Courtesy of William D. McDonald.*

Unusual E.C. Atkins & Co. heavy anvil block. Might have been used in a logging camp's filing shack. *Courtesy of William D. McDonald.*

Other side of Atkins anvil block. *Courtesy of William D. McDonald.*

Two Morin saw setting tools for use with a hammer to set the teeth on a two man crosscut saw. c. 1929.
$40-60 each.

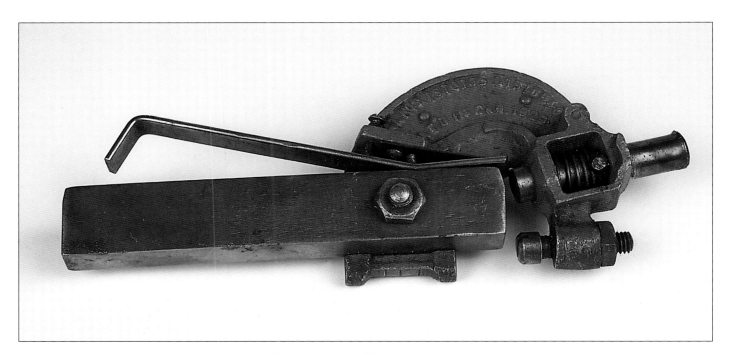

Anderson saw set No. 5. $40-55. *Courtesy of William D. McDonald.*

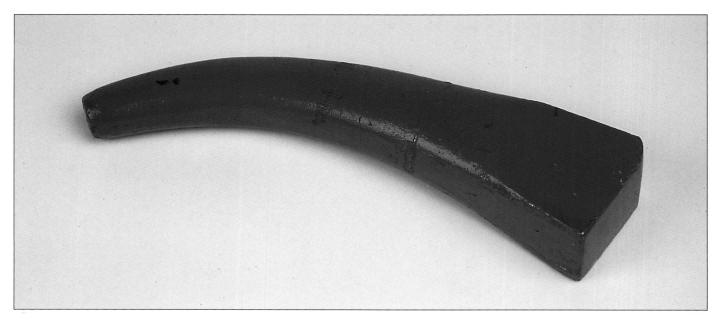

Atkins banana cutter tooth set anvil. $15-30. *Courtesy of William D. McDonald.*

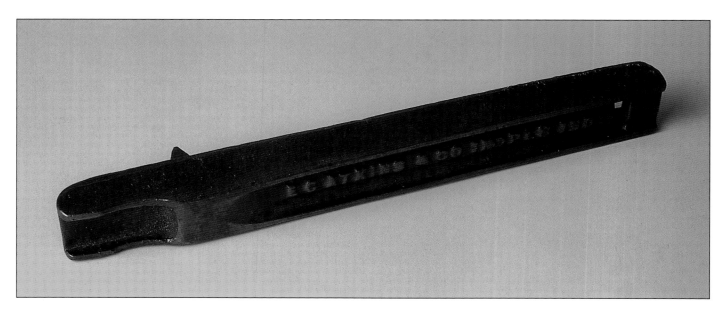

E.C. Atkins & Co. set stake. The stake is pounded into a log or other wood. A saw cutter tooth is set over the beveled end and set with a saw setting hammer. $15-35.

Saw filer working in logging camp. Cherry Valley Timber Company, c. 1920.
Photographer: Clark Kinsey. *Courtesy of Weyerhaeuser Archives.*

Two marked Doghead saw
filers hammers. Doghead
hammers range from 1 1/2
to 10 lbs. $75-125 each.

75

Close up of Doghead hammers. The E.C. Atkins is a 4 lbs. 6" head.
The Harper is a 4 1/2 lbs. 6 3/4" head.

Three saw set hammers with spring set notches. $30-60 each. *Courtesy of William D. McDonald.*

Close up of Simonds No. 337 saw setting hammer. *Courtesy of William D. McDonald.*

Atkins No. 4 saw swagging hammer. $45-65. *Courtesy of William D. McDonald.*

Two spring set saw tooth setting tools. One is marked Disston, the other has been decorated by a previous owner. $15-25 each.

A nice example of an Atkins Criterion saw setting tool with original box and instructions. $45-60.
Courtesy of William D. McDonald.

Simonds Raker gauge No. 342 with original box, instructions, set stake, and spider. $40-60.

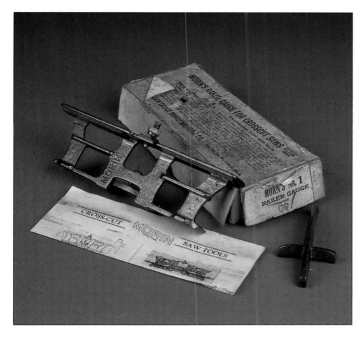

Morin No. 1 raker gauge made in Seattle, with original box, instructions, and spider. $25-40.

Two Anderson No. 1 raker swages. $15-30 each. *Courtesy of William D. McDonald.*

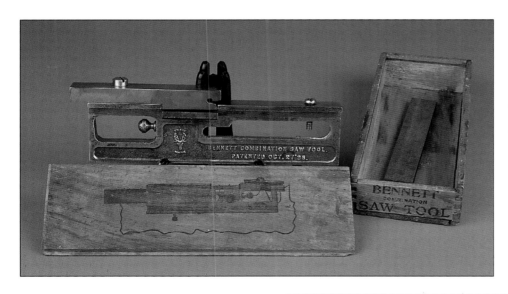

Uncommon combination saw tool by Bennett with wooden box. Pat. Oct. 27, 98. $40-65.

Three common raker gauges. $10-30 each.

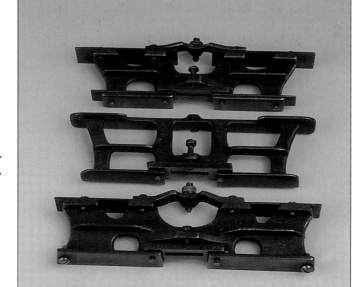

Two Anderson No. 4 raker gauges. $30-50 each. *Courtesy of William D. McDonald.*

Anderson raker gauge No. 3. $30-50. *Courtesy of William D. McDonald.*

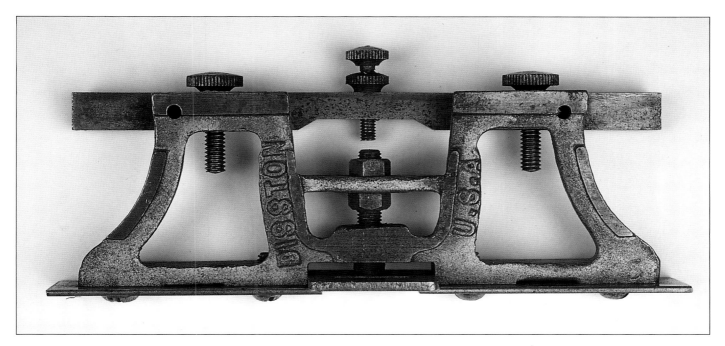

Disston raker gauge. $25-40. *Courtesy of William D. McDonald.*

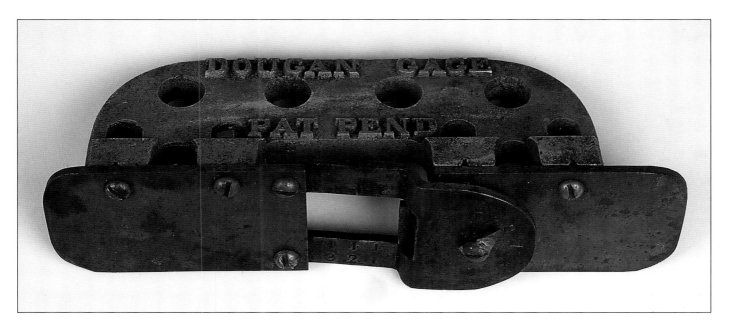

Dougan gauge, for drag saws? $30-50. *Courtesy of William D. McDonald.*

Three spider gauges. Used to check tooth set.
$10-15 each.

Uncommon Disston logo
shaped spider. $35-60.
*Courtesy of William D.
McDonald.*

Two Gibbs long jointers.
These long jointers are
a sought after filing tool
by collectors and saw
filers. $175-275 each.
*Courtesy of William D.
McDonald.*

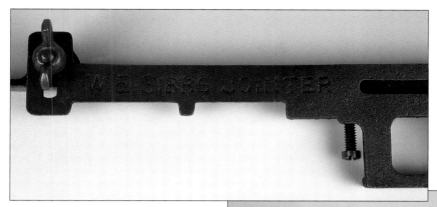

Close up of the writing on the Gibbs long jointer. *Courtesy of William D. McDonald.*

Close up of the patent dates stamped on the Gibbs long jointer. *Courtesy of William D. McDonald.*

Gibbs Raker Gauge for Cross-Cut Saws

Patented

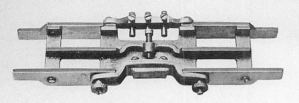

Directions for Use Packed with Each Tool

Three gauges in one, designed for those who want a perfect Tool. It will appeal particularly to the expert Cross-cut Saw Filer.

Price, $5.00 each

Gibbs Cross-Cut Saw Jointer

Patented

Directions for Use Packed with Each Tool

The only Tool of its kind. It will joint all makes of Cross-cut saws perfectly; instantly adjustable to any saw.

Price, $5.00 each

132

Simonds catalog illustration showing Gibbs jointers. *Courtesy of Simonds International.*

CHAPTER THREE

BOARDS, BOTTLES, AND METAL

In the Northwest, the springboard must have at one time existed in the tens of thousands, for every old stump in the woods seems to have at least a couple of springboard notches. Today they are not all that common; well-used examples are even harder to come by. The springboard was invented because the terrain in the Northwest is uneven and the easiest way for two fallers to be level with one another was to perch themselves off the uneven ground and above all that brush. Certain species of trees such as the western red cedar are wide at the base of their trunks, so loggers would set their springboards up to twenty feet off the ground to get at the narrowing portion of the trunk for a quicker cut. The logger in these cases would use two or three springboards. He would cut a notch, then place the first springboard, jump onto the springboard, and then cut another notch a few feet higher. Then the second springboard would be put into place and the logger would bury the axe deep into the tree and use the handle to help pull himself onto the next springboard while holding onto the third springboard with his other hand. The loggers spiked boots "corks" helped the logger perch on the springboards. The spikes bit into the wood, making it possible to balance on a springboard while swinging an axe or using a crosscut saw. There is not much to a springboard, just a four to five foot long board about seven inches wide, two inches at its thickest, and a triangular metal iron on one of its ends. A well-used springboard, with its chewed up surface from the spikes of the logger's cork boots, has personality like perhaps no other logging tool.

A logger would use an old whiskey bottle, a hook, a foot of wire or cord, and a stopper to make a valuable logging tool. The bottle was filled with kerosene to lubricate the saw and dissolve built up pitch. The logger used the hook to stick the bottle into the tree's bark for easy access. Usually the cork stopper that came with the bottle was replaced by a hand carved wooden plug with a notch cut along its length for the oil to drip out. The hooks were either bought from logging supply houses or were sometimes blacksmith made. The hook was attached to the bottle with a length of wire, twine, or cord and on later bottles with thumbscrew clamps. In the 1930s the twist on metal cap came on many bottles. The logger punched a small hole into the cap for the saw oil to dribble out when needed. The oil bottle represents simple ingenuity.

The bucker (the logger who would saw the fallen log into lengths) used certain tools that the faller did not; an "undercutter" is one of those tools. The bucker would have to sometimes cut the log from the underside up. The undercutter's stake was pounded into the side of the log and the back of the saw was placed on the grooved wheel. The undercutter provided support and leverage when sawing a fallen log from the bottom up. Loggers did not always pack heavy undercutters into the woods with them. They commonly used the ax handle as leverage for the saw. Undercutters come in different styles, including pocket undercutters, which were clamped onto the ax handle—thereby saving the ax handle from becoming grooved.

Both buckers and fallers used wedges. These wedges were used to keep the saw cut from closing and binding the saw. Logging wedges have a distinctive look. In the Pacific Northwest, falling and bucking wedges are only about one inch thick at their thickest. Eastern felling wedges are shorter and a little thicker. In the southern forests, hardwood wedges were frequently used. Falling wedges are longer than bucking wedges, and bucking wedges are wider than falling wedges. Logging wedges come in different weights and from different manufacturers. Some bucking wedges have a hole punched through them to tie two wedges together for carrying over a logger's shoulder.

Lumberjacks falling a huge fir tree along the Hoquim River. From the Wilhelm collection.
Courtesy of Tacoma Public Library.

SPRINGBOARDS

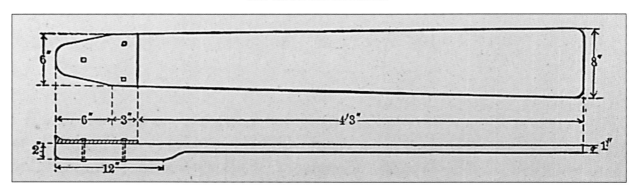

Early illustration showing the dimensions of a springboard.

Two long springboards, along with saws, axes, wedges, and sledge hammer for driving wedges. *Courtesy of Camp 6 Logging Museum, Tacoma, Washington.*

A nice example of a well used springboard. 5' long by 7 1/4" wide. The metal toe is stamped "Young," a Seattle, Washington, company. $125-200.

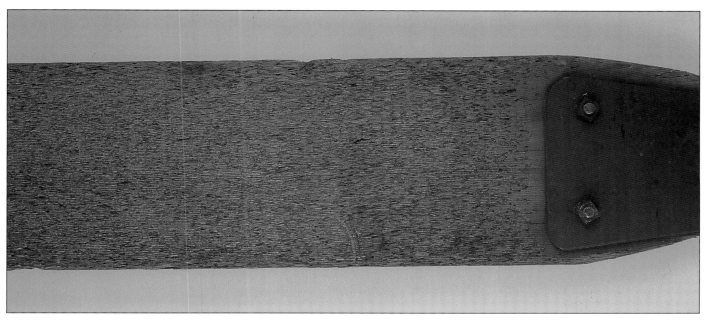

A close up of the springboard with chewed up wood from corks (loggers' spiked/calked boots).

USFS springboard and falling axe. $200-275 together.

Close up of stampings on springboard and falling axe. The springboard metal toe is stamped USFS and USFS is also burned into the wooden board. The falling axe is stamped FS in the head and USFS burned into the handle.

A nice and well used springboard with toe stamped "Young." Notice how the board is worn from where the logger would stand on the springboard. 65 1/2" long. $125-200.

Springboard with stain (possibly from broken saw oil bottle). 5' 2" long by 7 1/4" wide. The toe is stamped "Young." $150-200.

Notice how the board is thicker under the toe and thins out as it goes along.

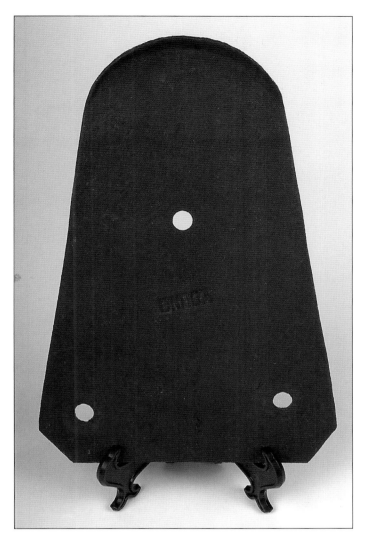

Young stamped springboard toe. The forward edge of the toe has a cleat that raises up about one half inch. The end of the springboard with the metal toe is used to fit into a notch cut into a tree. The cleat bites into the top of the notch when the logger stands on the springboard and keeps the springboard from slipping. $35-60. *Courtesy of William D. McDonald.*

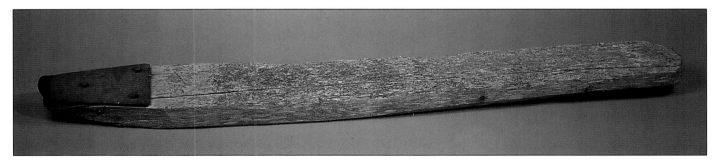

Courtesy of William D. McDonald.

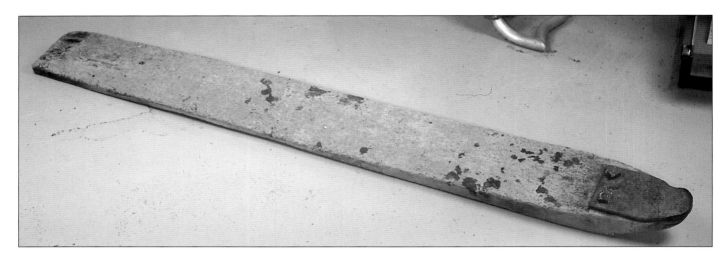

Courtesy of Ron Jones Power Equipment INC.

Courtesy of Mason County Historical Museum.

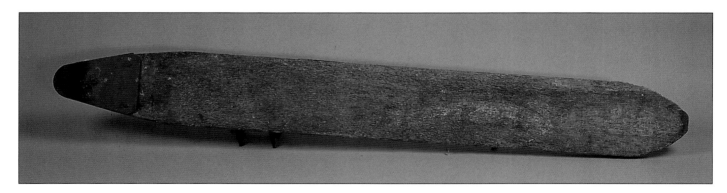

Courtesy of Mason County Historical Museum.

Courtesy of Mason County Historical Museum.

Courtesy of Mason County Historical Museum.

Two heavy springboards. Notice the split toe on these springboards. Sometimes blacksmiths would forge a springboard toe, also some manufactures offered split toe in their catalogs. $125-175 each.

Great old saw oil bottle with part of a blended whisky label. $50-100. *Courtesy of The Adams Family Collection, Elbe, Washington.*

Clear glass saw oil bottle with kerosene still in bottle, c. 1930s. $50-100. *Courtesy of The Adams Family Collection, Elbe, Washington.*

Old whiskey bottle with notched wood stopper. $50-100.

Two amber oil bottles with thumbscrew clamps, c. 1948. $45-95 each.

Green glass saw oil bottle with notched
wooden stopper.
$45-95.

This oil bottle has a screw cap with a small hole to dribble
saw oil. The bottle is stamped "Federal Law Forbids Sale or
Re-Sale of This Bottle." A piece of leather cushions the hook
against the glass. $45-95.

Screw cap top on this oil
bottle. Hook is wrapped with
a fine twine. $45-95.

Clear glass with wooden notched stopper. *Courtesy of William D. McDonald.*

Clear glass oil bottle with cord wrapped hook. *Courtesy of Mason County Historical Museum.*

This is a old whiskey bottle, old hook, and old logger-made wooden notched stopper. The wire however is new. The articles were put together to make a nice looking, but not completely original saw oil bottle. $25-45.

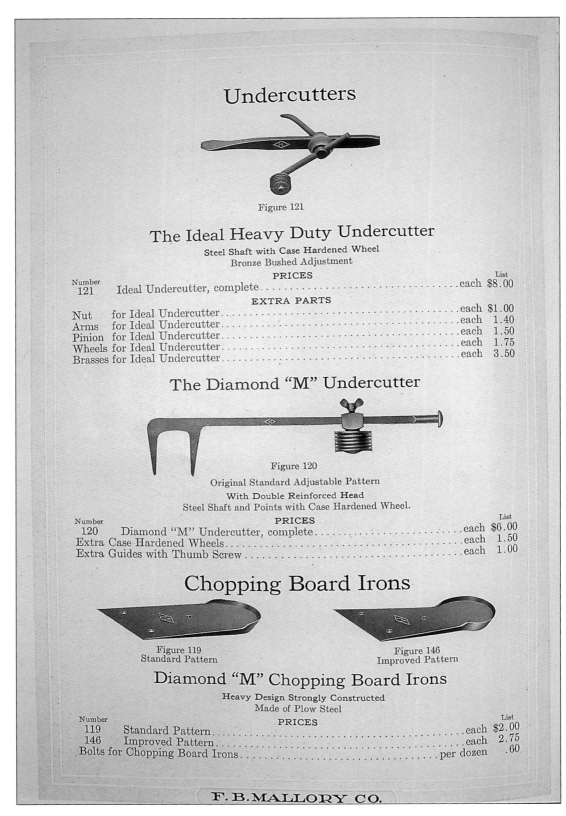

Undercutters

Figure 121

The Ideal Heavy Duty Undercutter

Steel Shaft with Case Hardened Wheel
Bronze Bushed Adjustment

Number	PRICES		List
121	Ideal Undercutter, complete	each	$8.00

EXTRA PARTS

Nut	for Ideal Undercutter	each	$1.00
Arms	for Ideal Undercutter	each	1.40
Pinion	for Ideal Undercutter	each	1.50
Wheels	for Ideal Undercutter	each	1.75
Brasses	for Ideal Undercutter	each	3.50

The Diamond "M" Undercutter

Figure 120

Original Standard Adjustable Pattern

With Double Reinforced Head
Steel Shaft and Points with Case Hardened Wheel.

Number	PRICES		List
120	Diamond "M" Undercutter, complete	each	$6.00
	Extra Case Hardened Wheels	each	1.50
	Extra Guides with Thumb Screw	each	1.00

Chopping Board Irons

Figure 119
Standard Pattern

Figure 146
Improved Pattern

Diamond "M" Chopping Board Irons

Heavy Design Strongly Constructed
Made of Plow Steel

Number	PRICES		List
119	Standard Pattern	each	$2.00
146	Improved Pattern	each	2.75
	Bolts for Chopping Board Irons	per dozen	.60

F. B. MALLORY CO.

Illustrations of undercutters and springboard toes. *Courtesy of Dr. Donald C. Jastad.*

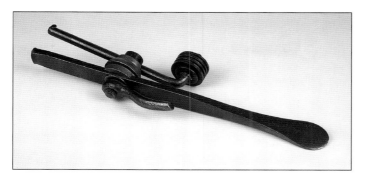

Ideal undercutter with brass knuckle parts. 17" long. $75-135.

Ideal undercutter. Much like the previous undercutter, but with a narrower point. $75-135.

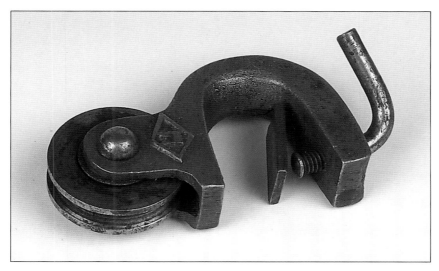

Mallory pocket undercutter for use on the handle of an axe. $145-200.
Courtesy of William D. McDonald.

Morin Pocket undercutter. Pocket undercutters are scarce and sought after by collectors. $145-200. *Courtesy of William D. McDonald.*

Undercutter with no maker markings. $65-125.

Unusual undercutter with two grooved wheels. $65-125.

27" long undercutter stamped "S&L"
with adjustable wheel. $65-125.

Two undercutters: Though undercutters in general are not common, this style of undercutter is found more often then any of the others. $65-95 each.

Large undercutter Gorilla/Stewart brand. $95-150.

Champion No. 1 undercutter. $85-135.

Undercutter with seven grooves on the wheel. As long as the logger has the undercutter in about the right position he can use the grooves for fine adjustment in positioning the saw blade. $65-125.

Undercutter with no maker's markings. $65-125.

Giant redwood with loggers posing for photo in undercut. Photographer unknown. *Courtesy of Mason County Historical Museum.*

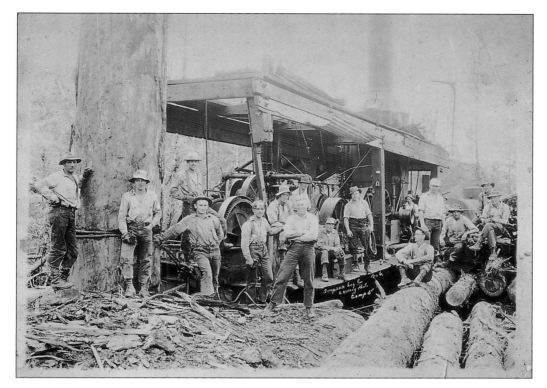

Simpson Logging Company, Camp 5. Photographer: Clark Kinsey. *Courtesy of Mason County Historical Museum.*

WEDGES

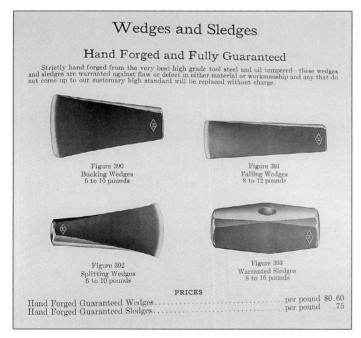

Illustration of Mallory wedges and sledge.
Courtesy of Dr. Donald C. Jastad.

Collection of falling wedges. These range in size from 12" to 16" long. $25-55 each.

Close up of falling wedges showing some of the maker's logos and weights.

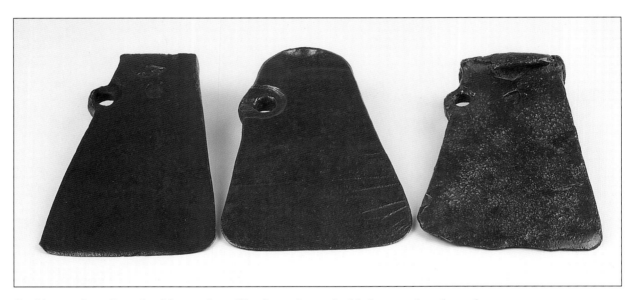

Bucking wedges. Some bucking wedges, like these shown, had holes punches through an upper edge so that a rope or wire could be used to tie two wedges together for easy transportation through the woods. $20-45 each.

Close up of Acme 6 lbs. bucking wedge with rope hole.

Pair of 6 lbs. Young bucking wedges with a rope, c. 1950. $35-65.

Long falling wedges with sledge hammer to drive wedges into saw cut. The wedges kept the tree from settling and pinching the saw. Wedges also helped to tip the tree toward the undercut. *Courtesy of Camp 6 Logging Museum, Tacoma, Washington.*

An 8 lbs. falling and 7 lbs. bucking wedge. Notice the difference in shape.
$55-75 a pair.

Close up of a pair of wedges, stamped "Skookum Heat Treated," along with their
weights, and a logo of a fir tree.

Four bucking wedges of different sizes. $15-35 each.

Eastern style wedge, 2 1/2 lbs. These smaller wedges were also used by high toppers. $15-35.

Gabriel 4 lbs. bucking wedge. $25-40.

Notice that a hole was started to be punched through, but was not finished.

Harmon wedge, Pat. July 9, 1912. These odd wedges were referred to as a glut. These wedges have a wood handle with a metal collar. Used to break cedar into bolts. $20-45.

A very large and heavy wedge. Stamped Clyde Equip. Co. This wedge weighs 10 lbs. $15-30.
Courtesy of Mason County Historical Museum.

Black powder blasting wedge. These were filled with blasting powder, pounded into a log, and a fuse inserted into the side hole. Powder wedges were used sparingly because the blast could waste the log. $65-125.

Black powder wedge. This particular powder wedge was used at a millpond. A rope and floats were tied to the wedge. The logs that were too big for the mill saw to handle had to be broken apart. The loaded wedge was pounded into the log, fuse lit, and after it blew the guys would jump into a row-boat to fetch the floats, pull up the rope, and retrieve their powder wedge. $65-125.

MARLIN SPIKES

Wire rope splicing exhibition. *Courtesy of Mason County Historical Museum.*

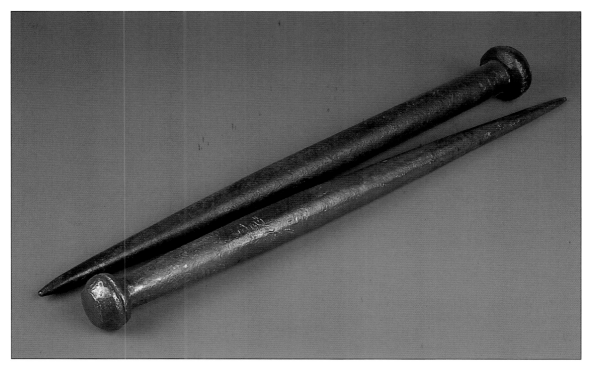

Two Marlin spikes, 21" long, used to splice logging wire cable/rope. $30-65 each.

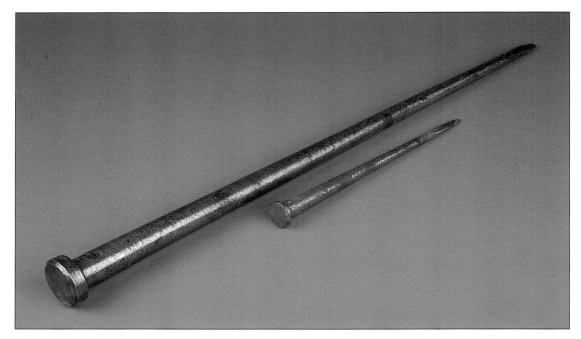

Two Marlin spikes showing varying sizes. The long one measures 24" long and the short one is 9 3/4" long. $30-65 each.

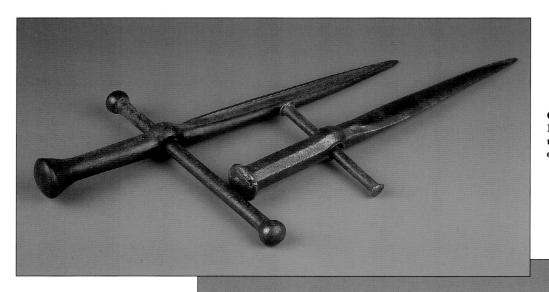

One flat and one grooved pattern Marlin spikes. These styles were used for splicing eyes and making other tuck splices. $40-80 each.

Knife made in logging camp out of wire cable.

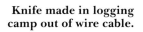

CHAPTER FOUR
PUSH, PULL, AND HOLD IT ALL TOGETHER

A number of tools were developed to push, pull, roll, and hold logs together. One of the most well known of these tools is the peavey. The peavey, used as a lever to roll logs either on land or in the water, is still commonly used to this day. Logs needed to be moved and all sorts of hooks, blocks, tongs, and jacks were produced, each one slightly different than the next.

Mason County Logging Co. Bordeaux Bros. Photographer: Clark Kinsey. *Courtesy of Mason County Historical Museum.*

Forest scene in Clallam County Washington near Port Angeles, c. 1903. Photographer: Leo Hetzel. From the Wilhelm collection. *Courtesy of Tacoma Public Library.*

Collection of boom chain, swamp hooks, loading hooks, logging dogs, choker hooks, falling and bucking wedges, boom augers, etc. *Courtesy of William D. McDonald.*

Ox yoke used in the early logging days. Swampers cleared the way through the woods, and buckers prepared the skids. A skid road was laid down with gentle curves and not too steep of a grade. Oxen yoked together in pairs and strung in teams that included as many as a dozen or more, slowly pulled giant logs over the skid road that snaked through the thick forest. 57" long and 14" deep in the middle. This yolk weighs 64 lbs. $300-400.

Two man yolk/timber carrier. In the early days of logging, two man yolks were used to carry the logs that were used in building the skid roads. $65-95.

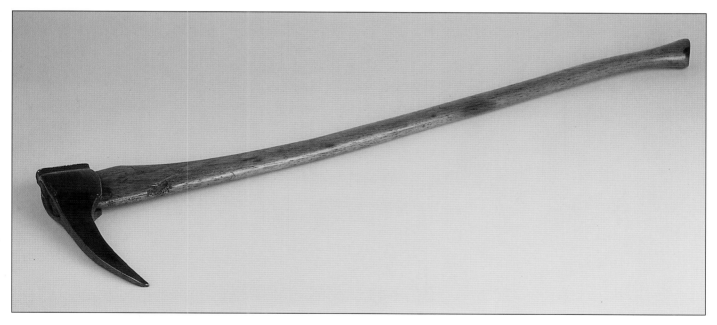

Pickaroon/Hookaroon. Used to muscle around smaller logs on land and could even work to move larger logs on waterways. $20-40.

This Pickaroon/Hookaroon has a light weight octagon fawns foot handle. $20-40.

Peaveys were, and still are, very useful tools for rolling logs. They were used in rolling logs in place for the skid roads, at mills, and on waterways. This Peavey is a big one, with a 8 lbs. socket head, 5' handle, and 3" in diameter at the socket. The head is stamped "A.M. Logging Tool Co. Evart Michigan." $50-90.

Port Blakely lumber mill showing sailing vessels at dock and a log pond in the foreground, Washington.
Courtesy of University of Washington Libraries, Special Collections, A. Curtis 19206.

Close up of Cant Hook. Notice how the end is designed differently than the Peavey.

Cant Hook. Used to roll logs, especially cants (squared off logs). $45-85.

Timber Jack. Mainly used to lift smaller logs/cants off the ground. $40-65.

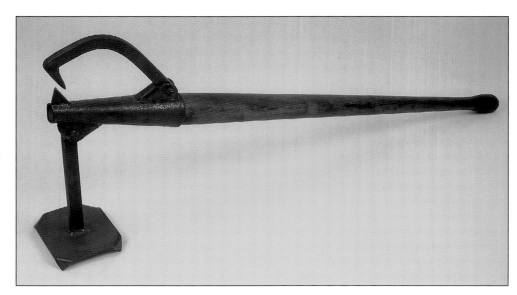

Pike Pole used on waterways to move floating logs around. Handles varied in length from 4' to 20'. This one has a handle measuring 12' long. $40-75.

Wood and metal log jack. $40-80.

Other side of early log jack.

Log loading/skidding tongs. Tongs vary in size. $45-85.

Rafting log dogs. These were pounded into logs on waterways and cable or chain swifter lines used to hold the logs together. $8-15 each.

Huge block pulley. *Courtesy of Camp 6 Logging Museum, Tacoma, Washington.*

Logging log dog hooks with chain. Used as general log dogs to pull logs. $40-70.

A slightly different version of log dog with chain set up. This set has a swivel in the middle of the chain. $40-70. *Courtesy of William D. McDonald.*

Logging log dog swamping hook, 20" long. $15-35.

Spar tree with rigging. Simpson Logging Company. Photographer: Clark Kinsey, c. 1925. *Courtesy of Mason County Historical Museum.*

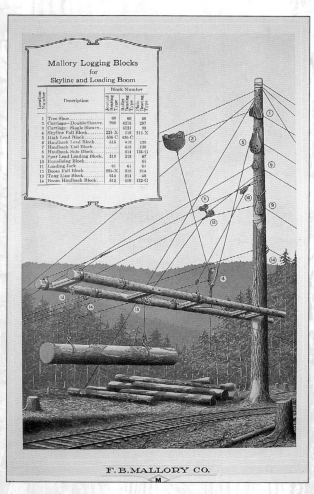

Illustration of Mallory blocks. *Courtesy of Dr. Donald C. Jastad.*

Chapter Five
Boots, Stamp Hammers, and Other Miscellany

One of the great aspects of collecting logging tools is that there is such an amazing assortment of intriguing objects to collect. When one thinks of logging tools, they might think of axes and saws, block and tackle, or steam donkeys. But there are all sorts of odds and ends that are related to the early days of logging. From loggers' calked boots, to vintage photographs, to stamp hammers, there are incredible numbers of items for the collector to explore.

Miss Pacific in hobnailed cork boots, c. 1954. From the Richards Studio Collection.
Courtesy of Tacoma Public Library.

Tall logging boots. The calks (spikes) gave stability when standing on fallen timber or high off the ground on a springboard. $30-60.

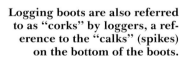

Logging boots are also referred to as "corks" by loggers, a reference to the "calks" (spikes) on the bottom of the boots.

Early pair of tall logging boots. Notice the lack of heel on these old boots. *Courtesy of The Adams Family Collection, Elbe, Washington.*

Leather sandal corks. Used by some workers instead of cork boots on millponds, rivers, and bays. The sandals were put on over shoes; that way if the worker fell into the water he did not have tall boots on that would fill up with water. $40-65.

Well worn wood and leather sandals. Loggers could wear their boots into some buildings such as bunk-houses, but not every business/home wanted loggers to wear their spiked boots across their floors. The logger would sometimes just leave their boots on and slip their boots into sandals so the floor would not end up looking like a worn springboard. $75-150.

Wooden whistle punk bugs used to signal the loader when the choker had set the logs and were ready to be yarded out. $45-80 a pair. *Courtesy of William D. McDonald.*

Close up showing the name of previous owner and the date of Nov. 11, 1936.
Courtesy of William D. McDonald.

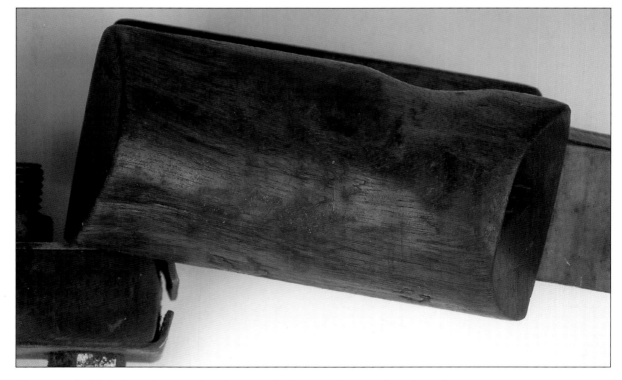

Close up of whistle bug showing thumb groove in the wood handle from lots of use.

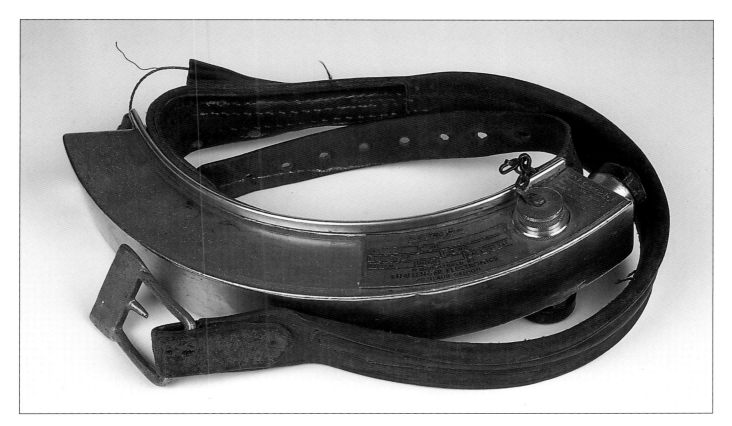

Electronic bug (remote radio). $35-55. *Courtesy of William D. McDonald.*

Spencer logger's tape measure. $15-35.

Recreated logger's bunkhouse.
Courtesy of Mason County Historical Museum.

Lantern and oil funnel
used in bunkhouses in
the early 1900s. $25-55.
*Courtesy of Mason County
Historical Museum.*

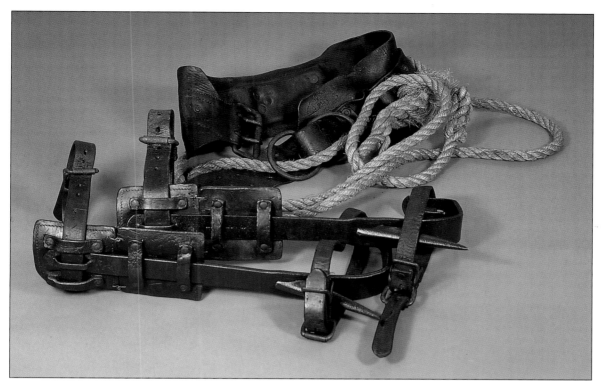

Climbing spurs and belt. The spurs attached around the climbers ankles and the long spikes bite into the bark. Not shown is a cable cored climbing rope that the high climber would wrap around the tree and use to help him climb. $65-110.

Oxen shoes and a rare oxen goad. The bull wacker was the guy in charge of the oxen. He encouraged the oxen along the skid road with words and the goad (a stick with a nail driven into one end). *Courtesy of Mason County Historical Museum.*

Cone shaped pole puller. Placed on a sniped log, the hooks driven into the log and a cable or horses used to pull the log. *Courtesy of William D. McDonald.*

Unused Norton axe stone. Loggers would carry axe stones with them into the woods so they could keep the edges of their axes sharp. $15-35.

Axe stone in original box. $15-35.
Courtesy of William D. McDonald.

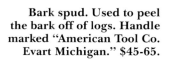

Bark spud. Used to peel the bark off of logs. Handle marked "American Tool Co. Evart Michigan." $45-65.

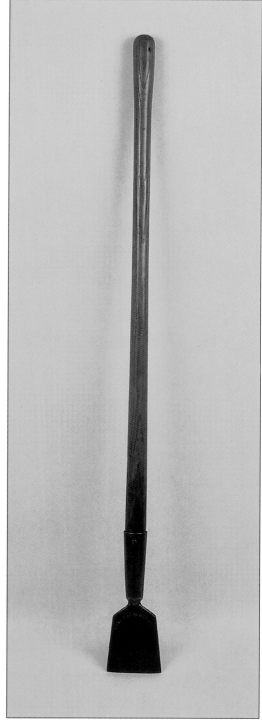

Close up showing stamping on bark spud. Marked "Warren Axe & Tool Co."

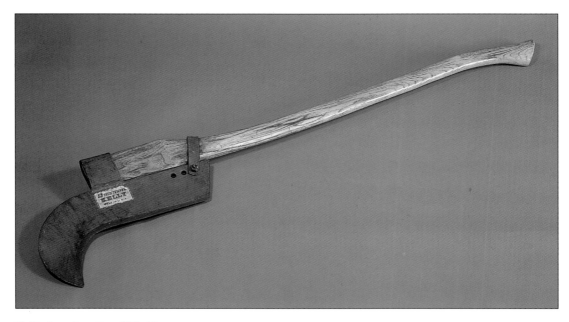

Kelly brush cutter. $25-45.

Topping a 200 ft. fir with Mount Rainier in the background. This Douglas fir would be used as a spar tree for St. Regis high lead logging operations, c. 1963. From the Richards Studio Collection. *Courtesy of Tacoma Public Library.*

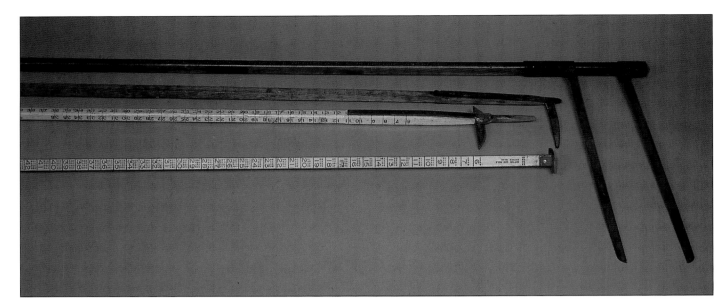

Scaling sticks/log rulers. There are a number of different styles, some of which were designed for specific uses such scaling logs on waterways. Different scales were also used, a few were Scribner, Doyle, and Spaulding. $45-85 each. *Courtesy of William D. McDonald.*

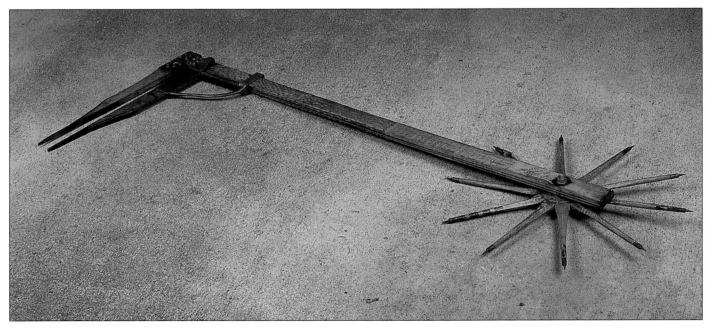

Eastern pin wheel scaling stick/log ruler. 46 1/4" long, pin wheel 20" across. $1000-1500.

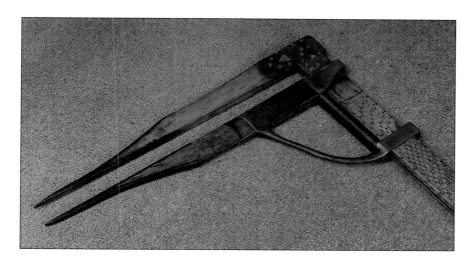

Close up of pin wheel scaling stick caliper.

Close up of pin wheel. Marked "G.E. Gould & CO. Littleton N.H. By GEK 1907."

Shipwright's lipped adze. Used in the logging industry for shaping the sleds (runners) of steam donkeys. Steam donkeys were steam powered engines with drums and cables used to pull logs to a central area "landing." Large wood runners were attached to the steam donkeys for the donkeys could be moved like a sled through the woods. They were used from the late 1800s to about 1950. $95-145.

Stump used to demonstrate log brands from log stamp/ branding hammers. The following hammers pictured are from the Pacific Northwest. Hammers used in the Great Lakes states and East Coast demand a higher price. *Courtesy of Camp 6 Logging Museum, Tacoma, Washington.*

Two similar log branding hammers using numbers inside of a border to brand the end of a log. $25-65 each.

Log branding hammer with a "W7" stamp. $25-65.

Log branding hammers come in different shapes and sizes. $25-65.

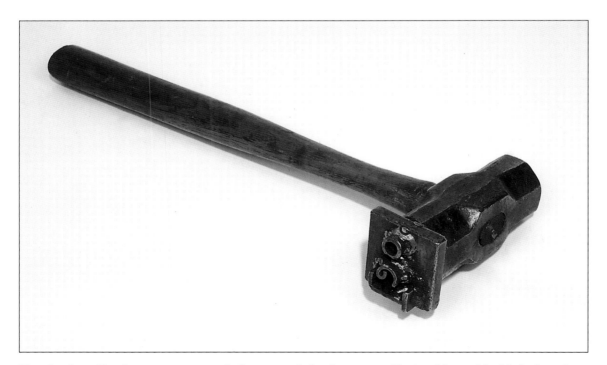

Most log branding hammers were made from an existing hammer, a blacksmith would add the brand to the poll of a single bit axe. $25-65.

Loggers McDonald hard hat, c. 1950s. $50-80. *Courtesy of Mason County Historical Museum.*

Early loggers hard hat. Loggers used to wear felt hats, then hard hats became standard, c. 1940s. $15-35. *Courtesy of Mason County Historical Museum.*

Vintage heavy logger's tin pants. These were made from an oil finished cotton. $30-50.
Courtesy of Mason County Historical Museum.

Early logger's lunch box. The top compartment held ice. If the logger could not make it back to camp for lunch, a boxed lunch had to do. $35-65. *Courtesy of Mason County Historical Museum.*

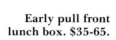

Early pull front lunch box. $35-65.

Later style lunch boxes. $20-45. *Courtesy of Camp 6 Logging Museum, Tacoma, Washington.*

CHAPTER SIX
DRAG SAWS
AND CHAINSAWS

The first chainsaws look like something Dr. Frankenstein might have created. There was no single style or look that all manufacturers used. The fact that the early chainsaws look so different from one another adds to their collectible allure. The following examples are a small representation of the number of early chainsaws produced. After WWII the number of chainsaws being used in the woods increased dramatically. Logging was going though a change that increased production and changed its methods. No longer were the axe and two man saw the tools that every faller and bucker used in their daily work. The chainsaw was an invention that, like the automobile, changed the status quo.

Adolph Frank was bucking logs at Grisdale when this picture was taken in 1948. The handsaw, the saw oil bottles, the steel wedges and the heavy sledge have about passed from the picture. And the steel hat has come in.

MUSCLES
Vs.
GASOLINE

Buck Lockwood demonstrates the modern way of power-sawing at Grisdale. He's felling an 8-foot Douglas fir with a one-man saw which snatches out chunks wood with the angry snarl of a hornet.

Poster showing the transition from whip saw to chainsaw. The men worked for Simpson Timber Co. Washington. The caption mentions Grisdale, which was the last operating company logging camp (1940-1985) in the lower forty-eight states. *Courtesy of Mason County Historical Museum.*

Simpson Logging Company Camp 5, showing early logging arch maneuvering through thick forest.
Photographer: Clark Kinsey. *Courtesy of Mason County Historical Museum.*

One of the first commercially produced chainsaws. This is an electric Wolf Link sawing machine, made in Portland, Oregon. Wolf produced this saw in pneumatic, DC electric, and eventually gas, c. 1920s. $150-500. *Courtesy of The Adams Family Collection, Elbe, Washington.*

Disston chainsaw advertisement. *Courtesy of William D. McDonald.*

Two cylinder Titan Blue Streak with stinger. Built in Seattle, Washington. $200-300.
Courtesy of William D. McDonald.

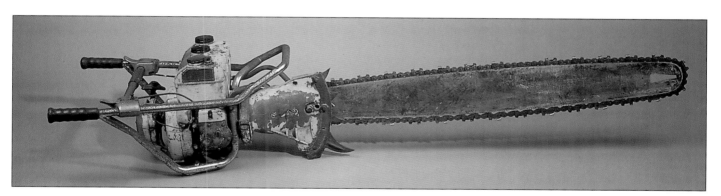

McCulloch model 99, c. 1952. $125-225. *Courtesy of William D. McDonald.*

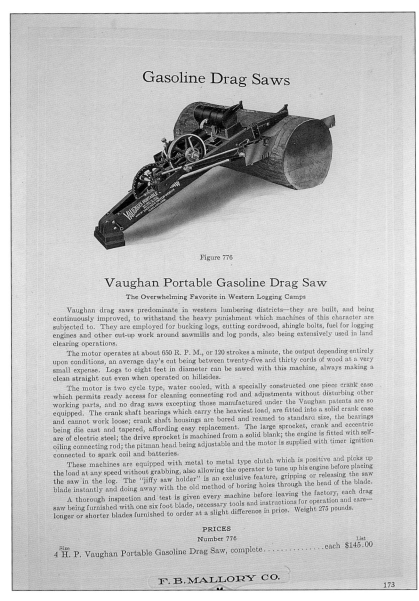

Illustrated advertising for Vaughan drag saws.
Courtesy of Dr. Donald C. Jastad.

Vaughan drag saw. Used to buck logs. $300-400. *Courtesy of William D. McDonald.*

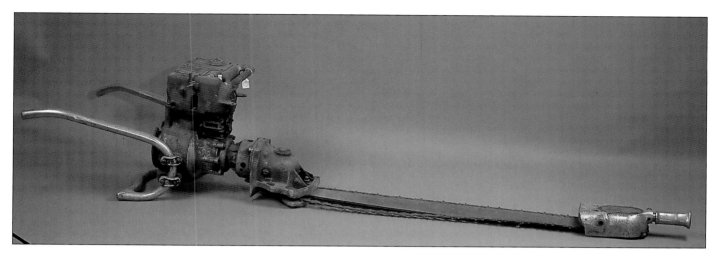

Two man Mall chainsaw 1949 model 10. A number of the vintage chainsaws had bars that rotated. Rotating the blade was necessary with saws used to fall and then buck a tree as the saw's engine would stall if tilted from its upright position. $150-300. *Courtesy of Mason County Historical Museum.*

Close up of Mall chainsaw. *Courtesy of Mason County Historical Museum.*

Titan with rotating bar, c. 1950s. $125-175. *Courtesy of Mason County Historical Museum.*

Fallers using a large electric chainsaw. Note the axe, or sledge handle, and oil bottle. Snoqualmie Falls Lumber Company, c. 1940s. Photographer: K.S. Brown. *Courtesy of Weyerhaeuser Archives.*

Mercury/Henry Disston saw. Quick stop in handle and chain straddles bar. $75-150.
Courtesy of Ron Jones Power Equipment Inc.

Close up showing Henry Disston & Sons logo on bar. *Courtesy of Ron Jones Power Equipment Inc.*

Poulan F 200 bow saw. Interesting saw used mainly to cut limbs. $150-200.
Courtesy of Ron Jones Power Equipment Inc.

Mercury two man with swiveling bar. $200-300.
Courtesy of Ron Jones Power Equipment Inc.

Close up of Mercury engine. *Courtesy of Ron Jones Power Equipment Inc.*

1944 two man Disston. $200-300. *Courtesy of The Adams Family Collection, Elbe, Washington.*

Remington chainsaw. $45-85. *Courtesy of Camp 6 Logging Museum, Tacoma, Washington.*

Two man Titan with long 9' bar and stinger helper handle, c. 1940s. $200-300.
Courtesy of The Adams Family Collection Elbe, Washington.

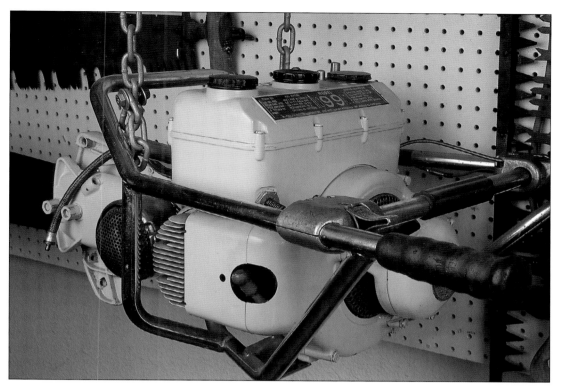

Very clean McCulloch model 99 with swiveling bar. $200-350.
Courtesy of Ron Jones Power Equipment Inc.

Close up of McCulloch logo. *Courtesy of Ron Jones Power Equipment Inc.*

R.M. Wade drag saw made in Portland, Oregon. $200-350.
Courtesy of Ron Jones Power Equipment Inc.

Close up of Wade drag saw engine.
Courtesy of Ron Jones Power Equipment Inc.

Close up of drag saw sprocket.
Courtesy of Ron Jones Power Equipment Inc.

Vintage chainsaws on display.
Courtesy of Camp 6 Logging Museum, Tacoma, Washington.

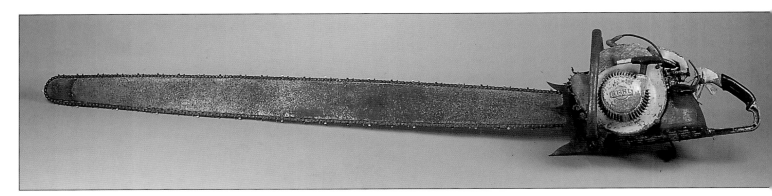

Early Stihl with a 5' bar. $65-125.

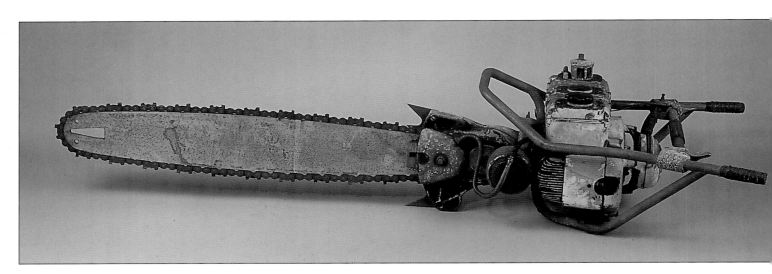

Early McCulloch Motors chainsaw. $125-195.

Vintage drag saw. *Courtesy of Camp 6 Logging Museum, Tacoma, Washington.*

Statue in Shelton, Washington, recognizing the workers of the wood working industry.

BIBLIOGRAPHY

BOOKS

Andrews, Ralph W. *This Was Logging*. Seattle, Washington: Superior Publishing Company, 1954.

Bryant, Ralph Clement. *Logging*. New York: Wiley, 1913.

Klenman, Allan. *Axe Makers of North America*. Victoria, B.C.: Whistle Punk Books, 1990. Second edition revised by Larry McPhail. Bellingham, Washington: Print & Copy Factory LLC., 2006.

Simonds. *Saws Knives Files Steel*. Worcester, Massachusetts: The Davis Press, 1923. Williams, Richard L. *The Old West: The Loggers*. Time Life Books, 1976.

CATALOGS

E.C. Atkins & Co. Inc. Catalog No. 10.

F.B. Mallory Company. Logging Equipment, Catalog Number Twelve. Portland, Oregon: Sweeney, Varney & Straub, 1925.

"Kelly Axe & Tool Works." *True Temper Kelly Quality, Catalog 30*. Cleveland, Ohio: The Calvert-Hatch CO.